CW01617485

ADVANC

WORD Processing

ADVANCING WORD Processing

Exam success at Stage III

Carol McKenzie
Pat Bryden

Heinemann

Heinemann Educational
a division of Heinemann Publishers (Oxford) Ltd,
Halley Court, Jordan Hill, Oxford OX2 8EJ

OXFORD LONDON EDINBURGH MADRID ATHENS BOLOGNA
PARIS MELBOURNE SYDNEY AUCKLAND SINGAPORE TOKYO
IBADAN NAIROBI HARARE GABORONE PORTSMOUTH NH (USA)

First published 1994

98 97 96 95
10 9 8 7 6 5 4 3 2

A catalogue record for this book is available from the British Library on request.

ISBN 0 435 453025

Designed by Ken Vail Graphic Design, Cambridge

Printed in Great Britain by Henry Ling Ltd, at the Dorset Press, Dorchester, Dorset

The authors and publishers would like to thank the RSA for their assistance.

Contents

About this book

Advancing Word Processing has been written as a continuation text to *Introducing Word Processing** and *Extending Word Processing*** by the same authors. It has been designed as a progressive course and is suitable for use in the classroom, in an open-learning workshop or as a private study aid.

Advancing Word Processing will help those preparing to take an advanced examination in word processing, using any suitable software package. However, the book would be equally useful to those who simply wish to extend their working knowledge of word processing.

Coverage

This book is designed for those of you preparing to take the RSA Stage III Word Processing examination. Units 1–4 cover Part 1 of the Stage III examination. Units 5–8 cover Part 2 of the Stage III examination.

Assessment

At the end of Unit 4, you should be able to complete an RSA Stage III Part 1 paper:

- **a** with in a *one-and-a-quarter-hour* time limit
- **b** with no more than ten accuracy and seven presentation errors for a *Pass*
- **c** with no more than three accuracy and three presentation errors for a *Distinction.*

At the end of Unit 8, you should be able to complete an RSA Stage III Part 2 paper:

- **a** within a *one-and-a-quarter-hour* time limit
- **b** with no more than six accuracy and four presentation errors for a *Pass*
- **c** with no more than two accuracy and two presentation errors for a *Distinction.*

Previous experience

It is assumed that you have completed elementary (Stage I) and intermediate (Stage II) word processing courses and are familiar with conventional document layout and text-processing principles and practice. You should also be familiar with the hardware you are going to use (including the printer).

Format

Units 1–3 and **5–7** take you through word processing functions you need to know for RSA Stage III examinations. Instructions for the preparation of particular documents are given at the beginning of each unit, followed by practice exercises.

Consolidation practice for each part of Stage III is available in Units 4 and 8, i.e., after all the topics for each part of each syllabus have been covered.

Print-out checks for all exercises are included in the book and these may be used for checking by both students and teachers/trainers.

The progress review checklist (see centre pull-out section) can be used to record progress throughout the use of the book – in learning and in accuracy.

* This publication covers the following syllabuses:
RSA Computer Literacy and Information Technology (word-processing application)
RSA Core Text Processing Skills (taken on a word processor)
RSA Stage I Word Processing.

** This publication covers the following syllabuses:
RSA Stage II Word Processing, Parts 1 and 2.

Command boxes for all word processing functions are inserted to show that you need to learn the commands relevant to your software in order to carry out a new word processing function. (At some points, command boxes relating to previously learnt functions have been included as revision.) These command boxes are intended as points of reference to draw your attention to the need to consult the glossary of commands.

The glossary of commands gives space alongside each function for the insertion of the appropriate software commands. Once the (pull-out) glossary is completed, you will be able to use it as a quick reference guide to functions and commands.

- If you are working on your own, refer to the software manufacturer's manual and insert the command sequence in the space provided against the command boxes in the glossary.
- If you are using the book as a tutor for a group of students, you could take a photocopy of the blank glossary and then insert the command sequences in the spaces provided against the command boxes. You could then photocopy the completed glossary for distribution to your students.

How to use this book

If you are preparing for an examination, you are advised to work through the book unit by unit. The book has been planned as a progressive course and some of the work you will do in the later units is based on text you keyed in earlier so it is important to save your work.

Using the glossary and the command boxes

The book has been designed for use with any word processing program, and command boxes have been inserted within the text and the exercises to indicate that you need to learn a new function. The command boxes are reproduced in the glossary so that a complete quick-reference guide is available. You learn the commands to carry out a new function as you work through the book. (See previous section on completing spaces in the glossary.)

Working through a unit

1. *When you see this symbol, read all the information* before you begin.
   You may also need to refer back to this information as you carry out the exercises.

2. *When you see this symbol, carry out the exercises* following the numbered steps, e.g., 1.1, 1.2.
3. *Use your program's spellcheck facility*, if available, to check your document.
4. *Proofread* your work carefully – spellcheck doesn't find every error.
5. *Use your preview facility*, if available, to check that your document is going to be correct when it is printed. This is particularly useful when you need to check headers, page numbering and justification as these features do not always show on the normal working screen.
6. *Save your work* on to your floppy disk (usually in A Drive).
7. *Call up the directory (or list of files)* of your disk on to the screen and *print your work* from this directory. (Although you may be able to print your work directly from screen, it is good practice, particularly when preparing for an examination, to print from the directory.)
8. *Compare* your work with the *print-out checks* at the back of the book. (If you are using this book in class, your tutor may also wish to check your work.)
9. *Exit* from the word processing program, or begin the next unit (as appropriate).

Do not delete files from your disk – you will need them later!

At the end of Unit 1, you will have learnt how to:

- **a** use apostrophes correctly
- **b** identify and correct errors of agreement
- **c** identify and correct typographical and spelling errors
- **d** produce a business letter in the fully blocked style
- **e** indicate enclosures and routeing on a letter
- **f** print a letter on A4 pre-printed letterhead
- **g** change pitch for a document
- **h** produce a business letter with a continuation sheet.

Apostrophes

At Stage III, you will be expected to know when to use an apostrophe and where it should be positioned in the word it relates to. An apostrophe is used to show that a letter (or letters) have been left out, e.g.:

don't	(*do not*)	haven't	(*have not*)
she'd	(*she had*)	you're	(*you are*)

1.1 Starting a new document, key in the following sentences, shortening the words underlined and putting the apostrophe in the correct place:

You are late! We have been waiting for you. Sit down and we will start or there will be no food left for you.

Do not say you cannot do the work. It is not difficult and there is no reason why you should not finish it.

(Leave this work on the screen. Do not save or print yet.)

More apostrophes

Apostrophes are also used to show possession – that something 'belongs' to someone or something, e.g.:

Nicola's pen	(*the pen of Nicola*)
The book's cover	(*the cover of the book*)
Tomorrow's paper	(*the paper of tomorrow*)
The day's work	(*the work of the day*)

If the word ends in 'ss', an apostrophe is added but there is no extra 's', e.g.:

The dress' zip	(*the zip of the dress*)

If there is more than one 'possessor' the apostrophe goes after the 's', e.g.:

The students' desks	(*the desks of the students*)
The girls' aunt	(*the aunt of the girls*)
The dresses' zips	(*the zips of the dresses*)

1.2 Key in the following sentences below the previous exercise, rearranging the underlined words and inserting the apostrophes in the correct places:

The glare of the sun caused the eyes of the player to lose sight of (the) ball of his opponent. The end of the game was announced and the victory of the winner was acknowledged by the captain of the other team.

The streets of the city were crowded as tourists and residents waited to see the car of the Mayor arrive at the entrance to the Club. The Freedom of the City was to be bestowed on the football team of the city and its manager.

(Leave this work on the screen. Do not save or print yet.)

Even more apostrophes

In speech, 'its' can mean two things: 'it is' (or 'it has') or 'belonging to it'. An apostrophe is used only when the full phrase of 'it is' (or 'it has') is shortened – the apostrophe shows that a letter has been missed out, e.g.:

It's good	*(It is good)*
It's said	*(It is said)*
It's up to you	*(It is up to you)*
It's been on my mind	*(It has been on my mind)*

But

The house has its door painted red.
We will improve its appearance.
The chair had its legs repaired.

1.3 Key in the following passage below the previous exercises, inserting apostrophes where necessary:

Its your decision as to whether you wish to bring the dog on Saturday. Its well-behaved and the children like its friendly nature. They were pleased to hear that its recovered from its recent illness and they are looking forward to its coming so that it can play with its new toys and they can see for themselves that its fit and well again.

(Leave this work on the screen. Do not save or print yet.)

Apostrophes again

Apostrophes are sometimes used in the plural (when there is more than one) of words that are not usually used in the plural, e.g.:

pro's and con's	60's and 70's
If's and but's	p's and q's

(*but* more and more frequently these words are shown without apostrophes).

1.4 Key in the following passage below the previous exercises, inserting apostrophes in the correct places:

We were always told to be careful to dot our is and cross our ts but the typewriter, which must date from the 1950s or 1960s, wouldnt print ws and ps and missed the tails off the ys, qs and gs.

1.5 Check your work on screen against the print-out check at the back of the book. If you have made any errors, refer to the explanations on the use of apostrophes in the unit, and amend your text on screen. There is no need to save or print this work.

Errors of agreement

This type of error will appear in the manuscript text which you are copying, and in retrieved text in the examination. The errors will *not* be circled at Stage III – you are expected to find these errors and correct them automatically as you key in the text.

As you are keying in text, you should make sure that what you are typing makes sense – 'listen' to what you are typing.

You should watch out for errors of agreement such as:

> This class of girls are irritating.

should be keyed in as:

> This class of girls is irritating

because there is only *one* class. If there were more than one class, you would key in:

> These classes of girls are irritating.

> The difference between the two word processing programs were demonstrated by the supervisor.

should be keyed in as:

> The difference between the two word processing programs was demonstrated by the supervisor.

because there are *two* programs but only *one* difference.

Typographical and spelling errors

The manuscript text which you copy will also contain some typographical and/or spelling errors. *Remember always to use your program's spellcheck facility before you print your work!*

Be careful of homophones, e.g.:

here	*and*	hear
their	*and*	there
course	*and*	coarse
are	*and*	our

Spellcheck will not find this type of error – it's up to you to read the text and choose the correct version.

Business letter on A4 pre-printed letterhead

One of the tasks in the RSA Stage III Part 1 examination is to *key in a business letter* and print it out *on an A4 letterheaded sheet.*

A letterhead has the name and address of the sender printed at the top of the sheet. Included in this book are three sample letterheads (see centre pull-out section). You could photocopy these and use them for practice.

In Part 1 of the Stage III examination, you can also expect to come across the following:

- **Complete business letter in fully blocked style.** As well as the reference and date, there will be a 'special mark', e.g., URGENT, PERSONAL, and a subject heading. The complimentary close will include the name of organization, and the name and designation of sender.
- **Enclosure and routeing to be indicated.** Enclosures should be indicated at the foot of the letter in the usual way. The text will mention a copy of the letter being sent to a named person or organization (routeing). To indicate routeing, leave at least one clear line after Enc(s) and type: 'Copy to' (*insert name of person or organization*).
- **Information to be located and inserted.** There are two possible sources of information to be inserted into a task:

  1 Another task in the examination paper.
  2 An announcement made by the invigilator. (Early in the examination, the invigilator will read out a piece of information which is to be incorporated into any one of the three tasks – *have a pencil handy so you can jot it down.*)

AUTOMATIC DATE FORMAT
Find out if your program has this function. It can save you time.

- **Abbreviations and unfamiliar words.** The RSA list of abbreviations is the same for Stage III as for Stage II (refer to *Extending Word Processing* (page 15) to refresh your memory). Copy all unfamiliar or foreign words carefully.

INDENT FUNCTION

- **Indented text.** A section of text (typescript or manuscript) may be indented for emphasis in any of the three tasks. You should retain the indentation, even though no specific instruction is given to you.

Producing a print-out on an A4 letterhead

It is the candidate's responsibility to print out the work in both parts of the RSA Stage III examinations. Your ability to print out this task and the method you use will depend on your printer. If you are taking an examination, you will need guidance from your tutor, or printer manual, on the following:

1 **The top margin to be used on your document.** Changing the top margin is one way of making sure that your printing starts at the correct point vertically on the printed letterhead.
2 **Feeding the paper into your printer and positioning it correctly (vertically).** Placing the letterhead in a particular position in the printer is another way of making sure that your printing starts at the correct point.
3 **Feeding the paper into your printer and positioning it correctly (horizontally).** The paper guide mechanism on your printer should be set so that when you print your letter, the left margin aligns as closely as possible with the printing on the letterhead.
Look at the print-out checks for Unit 1 and 4 to check the correct positioning of printing on a letterhead.
4 **Ensuring that the text at the bottom of your document will be printed on the letterhead.** Some printers do not print the last few lines of a document when single sheets of paper are being used. It is important that you find a way of solving this problem if it occurs on your printer because this task is usually a long one and takes up a full page.

MARGINS (to change)

Note: If you are working on your own without a tutor, you should experiment with this task to make sure that you can satisfy the requirements using your printer. Refer to your printer manual or manufacturer if you have difficulties.

Exercise 1A

1.6 Refresh your memory on consistency of presentation by referring to pages 10–11 in *Extending Word Processing*. Starting a new document, key in Exercise 1A. The information to be incorporated into your letter is Opportunities Unlimited. *Read the following points before you begin.*

Inserting your name and other details

It is usual practice in an examination to key in your name, centre number and the task number as Line 1 of a document. However, when the printing is to be done on a letterhead, these details are best positioned on the *same line as the date and flush with the right margin*, e.g.:

FLUSH RIGHT TEXT

12 December 1992 Your name Ex 1A

Changing 'pitch' in business letter

The letter may be a long one. You may be able to make the letter fit on one page by changing the pitch from 10 CPI (10 characters per inch) to 12 CPI (12 characters per inch).

PITCH (to change)

Before you print, move to bottom of document and check that document now fits on one page.

Exercise 1A

1.7 Starting a new document, key in the following letter. Save and print a copy of your work on an 'Opportunities Unlimited' A4 letterhead. Use the filename **EX1A**.

Letter to Mrs A Bottomley, 26 Hollings Way, BOROUGHTON, BB10 1WB. Mark PRIVATE please. Use ragged right margin. Save as EX1A and print a copy on an OPPORTUNITIES UNLIMITED letterhead. Use 12 PITCH so letter will fit on one page.

Dr Mrs B ______

'GOING IT ALONE' SEMINAR –
CAPS→ Sat (insert date for Sat. after next) (underscore all heading)

Further to yesterdays telephone conversation, I wd like ~~to let~~ give you have more info on the above event wh is aimed at providing prospective 'entrepreneurs' w the opp to acquire as much info as poss ~~in as short a time~~. as poss.

At O— U—, we ~~are very aware of~~ ack the fact that setting up in bus on yr own is an enormous step to ~~make~~ take ~~& it is important to have details of government and schemes wh could~~ we aim to help the budding businessman or businesswoman thro' the early stages. At the seminar, you wl be able to benefit from the knowledge and exp of local ~~leaders~~ leaders of bus & industry.

The day wl begin at 9.30 am w a talk by our Director, followed by approx one hour of presentations on currant "start-up" schemes. After coffee at 1100 hrs, the participants wl be invited to sep into small group & to pool there ideas & exps in considering what make a successfull bus. The afternoon wl be your chance to put yr idea(s) to an advisor and to rec individual advice. [I enclose a map showing the location of our temp accom, & a leaflet on the seminar. I have sent a copy of this letter to Ms P Farren, yr colleague. I look forward to seeing you ~~.~~ at the Seminar.

Yrs ffly

E A SUTCLIFFE
Conference Organiser

Exercise 1B

1.8 Starting a new document, key in the following letter, making all necessary amendments as you go along.

1.9 Save and print a copy of your work on a 'George Carter' A4 letterhead. Use the filename **EX1B**.

EX1B is to be printed on a letterhead. Please use a justified right margin. Mark the letter 'for the attention of the Health & Safety officer'.

RETAIN 10 PITCH

Baxter, Green & Co
Yates Quay
EASTPORT
ET4 7GH

A GOOD PLACE TO WORK?

The name of the factory is SEAVIEW ROAD

Dr Sirs

Thankyou for contacting me recently in response to our newspaper advert. //The GOOD P__ T_ W__? campaign began in (last month) of this yr and has def. recd a good response, both from employers and employees. The project employs 3 f/t workers, and approx 3 p/t assistants are used at each ~~venue~~ site to ensure info reaches local orgs. from the region

Our campaigns mobile caravan wl be in ~~yr~~ the Eastport area in (month after next) and, as you know, we are looking for a suitable sight to locate the caravan. It is necy for us to be in the bus centre of a town w suff car parking space for people to be encouraged to visit the exhibition without incon. Yr _____ factory wd appear to be ideal and I have written to yr Managing Director, requesting permission to use yr companys resources. I have send him a copy of this letter. JAMES GREEN, lower case

I enclose a brochure giving info on the exhibition and project and hope to here from you ~~soon~~ before (a week on Friday) so that arrangements can be finalised.

Yrs ffly

H HAMILTON
Project Leader

Letter with continuation sheet

The letter may be too long to fit on one page even if the pitch is changed to 12 CPI. In this case, the first page should be printed on the A4 letterheaded sheet provided and the second page should be printed on a sheet of A4 plain paper. You will have to decide where to insert a hard page break to form Page 2 and this page should be numbered.

Your name and exercise number should be printed on both pages. You could use any of the following methods:

NEW PAGE MARKER

Method 1: **Key in** your name and exercise number on Page 1 as previously instructed. **Key in** your name, etc., again at the top of Page 2.

Method 2: **Set a header** to print your name and exercise number at the *top right of both pages.*

Method 3: **Set a footer** to print your name and exercise number at the *foot of both pages.*

Exercise 1C

1.10 Retrieve the file **EX1B** and add the following text just before the paragraph which begins 'I enclose…'

It is very important that as many people as poss visit the exhibition in view of the fact that legislation ~~comes into force very soon~~ is already in place. The E___ C___ guidelines set out clear responsibilities for employers and employees alike and all managers/supervisors need to be made aware of ~~their~~ the part they must play in assessing workstations.
[It is, of course, no less vital that work practices are also examined w the aim of increasing efficiency + decreasing potential dangers and factors wh might promote disease and discomfort.

[We hope to dispel (DISPEL) some myths by giving factual info + advise based on thorough research.

(EC = European Community)

PAGE NUMBERING

1.11 Insert your name and exercise number using one of the methods described.

1.12 Set page numbering, suppressing this feature on Page 1.

1.13 Insert a hard page break in a sensible place.

1.14 Save and print a copy of your work. Use the filename **EX1C**.

At the end of Unit 2, you will have practised and revised all the text-editing techniques you have previously learnt.

Report or article

The Stage III Part 1 examination includes a report or article which may take up one or two pages. The task is to be keyed in by you and may test any (or all) of the items from the following list of word processing functions:

- ragged/justified right margin
- change of line spacing within a document
- insetting/indenting of text
- changing of line length
- moving blocks of text.

Refer to the glossary if you need to refresh your memory on the instructions for any of these word processing functions and commands.

The task may also test any of the following points of grammar and text-processing practices and conventions:

- errors of agreement
- typographical errors
- apostrophes
- RSA Stage III abbreviations
- manuscript correction signs.

Refer to Unit 1 if necessary. The RSA abbreviations were given in Unit 2 of *Extending Word Processing*.

Notes on consistency of presentation for measurements, weights, times, money, words and figures were given in *Extending Word Processing*. Notes on other possible inconsistencies are given on the next page for your revision and reference.

Points to remember

1. It is easier to set a header to show your name, centre number and task number when a document takes up more than one page.
2. Multi-page documents should usually have pages numbered – but not always the first page.
3. You should insert page breaks in sensible places.
4. Follow the usual procedures for making sure that your work is completely accurate – proofread very carefully, spellcheck and view before printing.

Other possible inconsistencies

You should be consistent in using the dash (-) or the hyphen (-) between words and symbols. The keyboard symbol is the same, but the spacing either side of the symbol is different. For example, don't key in **4 - 6** in one place and **16-21** somewhere else in the document. Also, don't key in **4 to 6** in one place and **16-21** somewhere else in the document. The word **to** can also be used, for example, in this way: **3 to 4 weeks' time, Tuesday to Thursday**. Don't key in **Friday - Sunday** in one place and **Monday to Wednesday** somewhere else in the document.

You should be consistent in the presentation of **per cent**. For example, don't type % in one place and **per cent** somewhere else in the document.

You should be consistent in keying in words which can be spelt in two different ways. For example, don't type **organise** in one place and **organize** somewhere else in the document.

CASE – TO SWITCH

Find out if your program can switch a block of text from upper case to lower case and vice versa. This can save you a lot of time when editing a document.

You should be consistent in the amount of space you leave after punctuation. For example, don't leave **1** space after a full stop in one place and **2** spaces after a full stop somewhere else in the document.

You should standardize the layout of any document which you are producing. For example, don't mix paragraph styles (e.g., keep them all blocked to the left *or* all indented) and make all headings the same style (e.g., all in capitals *or* all in lower case and underlined).

Exercise 2A

2.1 Starting a new document, key in Exercise 2A.

This leaflet draft is based on Exercise 1A. Refer to that task for any information you need

Ragged margin please

G— I— A— SEMINAR

(2 clear lines)

Saturday (insert date)

centre & underline

Opportunities Unlimited are ~~proud~~ pleased to ~~announce~~ organise this Seminar for prospctive business owners in the Boroughton area.

The Seminar will be held in the ground floor function suite and the programme for the day has been organized as follows:

Our offices are to be relocated ~~to~~ in the West End Business Park, where our new, ~~luxurious~~, purpose-built accommodation is nearing completion. In the meantime, we are fortunte that we have been allowed to use the premises of the ~~Stratton~~ Vendôme Hotel, High Street for ~~the~~ our Seminar.

double spacing

Introduction – 0900 hrs ← caps & underline

Neil Ross, Marketing Director of O— U— will ~~give an~~ outline the programe for the day & will introduce the speakers and reps (in full) from local industry, business & commerce.

1000 - Start-up Schemes

Presentations will be ~~presented~~ made by the High Street banks, the Small Bus Advisory Service & the British Franchise Association.

Topics will include: capital, loans, share issues, gov schemes and development boards.

Exercise 2A (continued)

1115 am – What Makes an Entrepreneur?

W the aid of case ~~studies~~ histories, participants wl be encourage to ~~talk about~~ discuss the viability of the respective businesses, types of bus organisation, market research, franchising, and employment law. The leader of each group wl advice on Income Tax, VAT & National Insurance. The aims is to make the participants more aware of the ~~many~~ pitfalls & pleasures of self-employment.

1100 hrs – Coffee

12.45 pm – Lunch in Carnery 1st floor

1400 hrs – Consultation ~~& Advice~~ Sessions

The 'experts' wl make themselves available for individuel consultation. Every participant can put his or her idea foreward and rec valuable assistance.

1600 hrs – PLENARY SESSION/PRIZE PRESENTATION

N— R—, Marketing D——, will ~~give~~ present an award – '____________' – together w a check for £250 to the 'entrepreneur' w the most originae (and viable) bus proposal.

The award wl be called 'Business Idea of the Day'

(The winner wl be ~~selected~~ chosen by all the expert present at the Seminar.)

Indent ½" at left and right

Save as EX2A and print one copy

Exercise 2B

2.2 Starting a new document, key in exercise 2B.

Please use justified margin, standardise layout and put 1st and last paras in double spacing. Use a line length of 55. Save as Ex2B.

A GOOD PLACE TO WORK? ← spaced caps } centre & bold

An Exhibition for Office Workers

The Information Tecnology revolution has changed the way we work and brought ~~with it~~ many benefits - both from the employers point of view and the employees angle. ~~Whilst~~ Altho' there are no serious occupational dangers such as you might find in an engineering workshop or a foundry, the office does have its own risks.

(underline paragraph headings and use lowercase)

MANAGERS/SUPERVISORS Do you know what your responsibilities are under EC legislation?

ELECTRONIC OFFICE WORKERS/VDU OPERATORS Do you suffer from eye strain, aching shoulders, (back pain) headaches? What can you do to make your working day more comfortable? How can your ~~firm~~ employer help?

↕ 3 clear lines where this symbol is shown

VISIT THE GOOD PLACE TO WORK EXHIBITION

~~Learn how to~~ Help yourself to a better workpalce } centre & bold

↕

It will be your job to assess every workstation ~~under~~ in your section/department. Its up to you to make sure EC recommendations are met.

The exhibition will offer:

- I_____ Vidio (Inter-active)
- Slides
- Displays
- Quizzes, Questionnaires
- Proffessional Advice

The person to ask for on 'phone is: HAMISH HAMILTON

Exercise 2B (continued)

~~We can advise on~~ 3 areas ~~of concern~~ of interest] CAPS, centre, no underline
Learn about

Health

Eye problems, muscular strain, repetitive strain injury, VDUs & problems w pregnancy. Is it really the computers fault?

What can be done to ~~alleviate~~ remove stress, worry and strain?

Ergonomics Workstations, systems, the workplace ~~as a whole~~ environment. Its ~~often easy~~ usually easy to change some aspects ~~eg~~ such as chairs, desks, & lighting but its more difficult to change the way we think and work!

This is a very extensive topic – you'll be surprised whats involved.

SAFETY Electricity, radiation, chemicals.

Expediency can ~~mean~~ lead to inadequate and dangerous practises in use of electricity. There are many toxic chemicals in offices (but theres no risk provided due care is taken).

We'll give you the ~~facts~~ evidence about radiation from VDUs.

Exhibition ~~opens~~ starts at 1000 hrs Mon-Sat & closes at 6pm Mon-Fri. (Early close Sat 1600 hrs.) Phone 071-124367 for exact location in yr town - ask for _____.

A G__ P__ T__ W__? ← spaced caps } Centre & bold

Appearing soon in a Car Park near you! ← CAPS

At the end of Unit 3, you will have learnt how to:

a complete a multi-page document using advanced features
b enter the command sequence for printing a text footer with automatic page numbering
c use 'quick' copy/delete/move commands.

Multi-page documents

In the Stage III Part 1 examination, the 'header and footer' task usually extends to four pages. Refer to the glossary for instructions on setting headers, footers and document pagination.

You may be required to carry out any or all of the text-editing techniques you have previously learnt, but the instructions will be more complex and varied.

Read through the task before you attempt any reformatting procedures. Ensure you understand all the instructions and amendment signs, and that you don't miss any.

Method of working

The following is a method of working that has proved successful and you might like to adopt. Using this method means that you will return to the top of the document and work through it several times, carrying out a different function each time. This might seem time-consuming but if you always use the method you will get into a routine and you will be sure that you have not missed anything out. There is an added advantage in going through a document several times – you might spot an error that can be corrected as you scan through the work!

Make sure you know how to move the cursor around your document as quickly as possible!

1 Set the header(s) as requested in the draft. Check if you need to put on page numbering, starting from Page 2, as well as any specified text footer – ensure that these do not overlap. Use preview facility to check that any header, footer or page number is correctly positioned.
2 **Spellcheck** and **proofread** the retrieved text* – there are usually many errors in this text.
3 Carry out all the necessary **text amendments**, e.g., inserting or deleting of text *throughout the whole document*.
Check carefully for abbreviations, spellings, errors of agreement, grammatical errors, consistency of presentation, typing errors, punctuation errors, etc. (within the retrieved text and the text you key in).
4 **Move blocks of text** and **copy blocks of text** as requested *throughout the whole document*.
5 **Search and replace text** as requested.
6 **Allocate space** and **indent** or **inset margins** as requested.
7 **Paginate** your document as requested or as you think fit (*read the instructions*).
8 **Spellcheck** the whole document using your program's spellcheck facility if it has one.
9 **Proofread** the whole document, comparing it word for word with the copy.
10 **View** your document using your program's preview facility, if it has one, to make sure that it is going to be printed correctly.
11 And finally **print** your work.

* The RSA Stage III Part 1 examination requires candidates to proofread not only their own keyed-in work but *also the retrieved text*. There are often spelling and grammatical errors in the text which has been keyed in prior to the examination by the tutor. Candidates should spellcheck and proofread the retrieved text very carefully indeed. This may be done before starting the task.

Footer command for automatic page numbering with text

If you need to show automatic page numbering *with text*, e.g., **Page No 1, Page 2** etc., you may not be able to use your software program's standard command for page numbering.

FOOTERS (with automatic page numbering)

The hash sign (#) is often used to symbolize automatic page numbering. (*Note:* On some programs you need to set the page number and text, e.g., Page no 1, via the footer command in conjunction with a special code or symbol to denote the page number – check with your tutor or manual. If your program has a standard page-numbering method, make sure this is not turned on at the same time as you enter the footer or you may get two sets of numbers printed on the page – again, check with your tutor or manual.)

3.1 Practise operating the footer command to put on automatic page numbering with text. Retrieve **EX2B**. Enter the command: **Page number** # at bottom centre of the page.

If your program has a preview facility, check the document on screen to make sure the footer command you have entered is correct, and that **Page number 1** is shown at bottom centre of the first page and **Page number 2** is shown at bottom centre of the second page. If you do not have a preview facility, print two pages for checking.

There is no need to save your work.

'Quick copy/delete/move' a block of text

With most word processing programs it is possible quickly to copy, delete or move blocks of text using a set command sequence. This will allow you to copy/delete/move either a sentence, paragraph or whole page using one 'quick' command. The RSA Stage III Part 1 examination requires a high degree of accuracy and a fast production rate. Find out about any quick methods available on your program which, after practice, may speed up your rate of production – refer to your tutor or manual. (*Note:* Not all word processing programs have these facilities.)

QUICK COPY/DELETE/MOVE

Exercise 3A

3.2 Retrieve the file **EX2A**. Look carefully at Exercise 3A – you are asked to make a number of amendments to the document including move, copy, delete, change line spacing, margin justification, search and replace, header, footer, and page numbering. Because of the existing format of the task you have retrieved, it would be easier to delete all the existing formatting codes (line spacing, justification, page numbering, etc.) *before* you attempt to redesign the layout. Please note that it will not be necessary for you to do this in the RSA III Part 1 examination. Work you way through the document, following the method of working described earlier, deleting any preset codes for line spacing, justification and page numbering.

As Exercise 3A is a multi-page document you will need to put on page numbering, starting from Page 2, as well as the specified text footer at the left-hand side of every page. To do this carry out steps **a** and **b** below:

a Using the footer command, enter the text reference **REF: OU/SH** at *bottom left* of every page

b Using your program's standard method of page numbering, set the page-numbering position to be at either *bottom right* or *centre* of page (remember to suppress page numbering for Page 1). *The instructions for this task ensure that the page number does not overlap with the text reference at bottom left. You need to be aware of this when creating your own layouts.*

Carry out all the amendments shown in Exercise 3A very carefully. Have you completed all the steps in the method of working given above?

Save and print a copy of your work – use the filename **EX3A**.

Exercise 3a

GOING IT ALONE SEMINAR (this line in spaced caps)

Saturday (correct date inserted)

Opportunities Unlimited ~~are~~ is pleased to organise this Seminar for prospective business owners in the Boroughton area.

NB: Our offices ~~are~~ are to be relocated in the West End Business Park, where our new, purpose-built accommodation is nearing completion. In the meantime, we are fortunate that we have been allowed to use the premises of the ~~Stratton~~ Vendôme Hotel, High Street, for our Seminar.

(please move this paragraph to Ⓐ and put in single line spacing)

The seminar is the first of it's kind in the area & shd attract much publicity from the media. We are hoping to organise suitable press coverage, eg the local newspapers.

The required fee for the full day will be seventy-five pounds ~~not~~ including lunch.

The Seminar will be chaired by Neil Ross, Marketing Director of O—— U——.

(indent these 2 paragraphs by 3" (75mm) at right margin to allow for a photograph)

Use a JUSTIFIED margin throughout the document
Use single linespacing except where specified differently
Use the header: BUSINESS SEMINAR at top right of every page
Use the footer: REF: OU/SH at bottom left of every page and number the pages at bottom centre starting from page 2
KEEP PAGE BREAKS AS SHOWN

All this page to be in DOUBLE LINE SPACING please

Exercise 3A (continued)

(This line in CAPS)

The ~~Seminar will be held in the ground floor function suite and the~~ programme for the day has been organised as follows:

0900 HRS - INTRODUCTION

Neil Ross, Marketing Director of Opportunities Unlimited will outline the programme for the day. ~~and~~ he will then introduce ~~the~~ speakers and representatives from local industry, business and commerce, including:

1 Mr ~~David Wetherby~~ Ahmed Kahn - CHAIRMAN Ridings & Holt Ltd

2 Mr Paul Knight - MANAGING DIRECTOR Vernons & Hoyle Ltd

3 Ms ~~Gladys~~ Gloria Fairway - MANAGING DIRECTOR Century Systems

4 Mrs Vanessa Debarry - SOLICITOR Mayes, Drew + Smithies

(indent by ½" (13 mm) at left and right margins)

(align the dashes)

1000 HRS - START-UP SCHEMES

Presentations will be made by the High Street banks, the Small Business Advisory Service and the British Franchise Association.

Topics will include: ~~capital, loans, share issues, government schemes and development boards~~.

1100 HRS - COFFEE

(operator: please put all enumerated items in single line spacing but with one clear line between items)

i) Capital
ii) LOANS
5 ~~iii)~~ Share Issues
iv) government Schemes
3 ~~v)~~ Development Boards
vi) Organizational Skills

There will also be a short talk from Mr Alan Stevenson ~~from the~~ who will advice on help available thro' various Gov start-up schemes, e.g. financial assistance, administrative support etc.

Exercise 3A (continued)

1115 HRS - WHAT MAKES AN ENTREPRENEUR?

divided into groups &

With the aid of case histories, participants will be encouraged to discuss the viability of the respective businesses, types of business organisation, franchising, market research, and employment law. The ~~leader of each group~~ will ~~advise~~ on Income Tax, VAT and National Insurance. The aim is to make the participants more aware of the pitfalls and pleasures ~~of~~ self-employment.

which come with

speakers for each topic

lead a 45-minute debate

The groups will then have an ~~[illegible]~~ opp to put foreward the main points from there discussions, including ~~and~~ any particular questions which remain unanswered.

(B)

leave 15 clear line spaces here

~~1245~~ HRS - LUNCH IN 1ST FLOOR CARVERY

1.00 pm

Exercise 3A (continued)

1400 HRS - CONSULTATION SESSIONS

The 'experts' will make themselves available for individual consultation. Every participant can put forward his or her idea and, in return receive valuable assistance along w constructive criticism.

1600 HRS - PLENARY SESSION/PRIZE PRESENTATION

Neil Ross, Marketing Director, will present an award - 'Business Idea of the Day' - together with a cheque for £~~250~~ 175.00 to the 'entrepreneur' with the most original (and viable) business proposal.

> (The winner will be chosen by ~~all~~ the panel of experts present at the Seminar.)

this sentence in CAPS and DOUBLE LINE SPACING – retain indented style

leave at least 10 clear line spaces here

Their will be a short 10-minute interval halfway through this session.

USE A LINE LENGTH OF 46 FOR THIS PARAGRAPH AND DOUBLE LINE SPACING. COPY IT TO (B) – USE THE SAME SETTINGS

(A)

Replace the name Neil Ross with the name Adam Flynn ~~thru~~ throughout the document

Exercise 3B

3.3 Starting a new document, retrieve the file **EX2B**. Refer to the exercise headed **Exercise 3B** and follow all the instructions carefully.

Save and print a copy of your work – use the filename **EX3B**.

Exercise 3b

Change to a RAGGED right margin throughout
Use SINGLE LINE SPACING unless specified otherwise

A G O O D P L A C E T O W O R K ?

An Exhibition for Office Workers

copy this line to *

The Information Technology revolution has changed ~~the way we work~~ our working lives and brought ~~many~~ numerous benefits - both from the employer's point of view and the employees' angle. Although there are no serious occupational dangers (such as you might find in an engineering workshop or a foundry) ~~the~~ office ~~does have its own risks~~ environment. There are still risks involved for those who work in an

single line spacing

Managers/Supervisors Do you know exactly what your responsibilities are under EC legislation?

It ~~will be~~ is your job to assess the safe working order of every workstation in your section/department. It's up to you to make sure EC recommendations are met.

Electronic Office Workers/VDU Operators ~~Do~~ If you suffer from eye strain, aching shoulders, back pain, headaches you should ask the following questions 1) What can you do to make your working day more comfortable? 2) How can your employer help?

3) Are you taking suff breaks away from the VDU screen
4) Is the office furniture adequate, eg chair set to correct height and w a backrest?
5) Is the air-conditioning affect we?
6) Have you had your eyesight checked by an an optician since you started working on a V.D.U.?

New gov laws are now in effect wh regulate the no of hrs an operator may sit at a VDU without a brake.

OPERATOR: keep this section together as Page 1

indent enumerated items 12 spaces from left margin & use single line spacing with one clear line space between items – use same style for any other enumerated items in document

Exercise 3B (continued)

VISIT THE GOOD PLACE TO WORK EXHIBITION

Help yourself to a better workplace

(this line in CAPS) (move this section so it becomes page 3 – leave rest of page blank)

The exhibition will offer:

a) Inter-active Video
b) Slides
c) Displays
d) Professional Advice from the many experts who will be on hand to deal w yr individual problems
e) Quizzes, Questionnaires

There will also be an Information Stand offering advice on EC Legislation.

THERE WILL BE CONTINUOUS LECTURES
~~LEARN~~ ABOUT 3 AREAS OF INTEREST:

Health Eye problems, muscular strain, repetitive strain injury, VDUs and pregnancy. ~~Is it~~ Are all health problems really the computer's fault? What can be done to alleviate problems w stress, strain and worry?

Ergonomics Workstations, systems, the workplace environment. It's usually easy to change some aspects such as chairs, desks, and lighting but it's more difficult to change the way we think and work!

This is a very extensive topic – you'll be surprised what's involved. (you will – in full)

OPERATOR!

* use the header EXHIBITION at top right
* use the footer OFFICE WORKERS at bottom right
* number the pages at bottom left starting on page 2
* follow the instructions given for page breaks

Exercise 3B (continued)

(keep this paragraph on the "...... 3 AREAS OF INTEREST page)

<u>Safety</u> Electricity, radiation, chemicals. Expediency can lead to inadequate and dangerous practices in the use of electricity. There are many toxic chemicals in offices (but there's no risk <u>provided</u> due care is taken). We'll give you the facts about radiation from VDUs. (– 95% of accidents are caused through negligence)

(OPENING TIMES – Insert as a heading where shown and start a new page (p 4). Use DOUBLE LINE SPACING for all of page 4)

Exhibition opens at ~~1000~~ 9.30am hrs Monday - Saturday and closes at 1800 hrs Monday - Friday. (Early close Saturday 1600 hrs.) Phone 071-124367 for exact location in your ~~town~~ area - ask for Hamish Hamilton.

Admission fee: £1.00 Adults
£0.50p Children (accompanied)
fifty pence OAPs

Parties of 10 or more qualify for a ten per cent discount.

(please set line length for this section only to 46)

(leave 7 clear lines here)

A G O O D P L A C E T O W O R K ?

APPEARING SOON ~~IN A CAR PARK~~ NEAR YOU! (centre)

OPERATOR: replace the abbreviation EC with European Community throughout the document

Printing-out arrangements

Printing-out arrangements in the RSA Stage III Part 1 examination

You are given 10 sheets of A4 paper and two pre-printed 'Praxiteles' letterheads in this examination. *(Put your letterheads on one side to ensure they are not used for draft printing.)* This is sufficient to be able to print out the following:

- 1 *final* copy of the 2-page document
- 1 *final* copy of the 4-page document
- 1 *final* copy of the letter on letterhead.

You will then have four sheets of plain paper with which to print draft copies during the examination. The letter may take one or two sheets so if you print a draft copy, you will then have to decide to use the remaining two or three sheets in one of the following ways:

1 Print a draft copy of the two-page document.
2 Print a draft copy of *one page* of the two-page document *and* a draft copy of *one page* of the four-page document (*to check headers, etc.*).
3 Print a draft copy of *two pages* of the four-page document.

You should make sure that you have practised printing on letterheads using the same equipment that will be available for your examination and RSA's Praxiteles' letterheads.

The printing of the final copies of the tasks in this examination is done outside the examination time of one and one-quarter hours *by the candidate.*

No amendments may be made to the text after that time has expired and the printing should be done from the list of files (or directory) screen. (*There is no need to retrieve the document to print.*)

You are allowed to insert special characters, such as accents, on to the final copies after the examination time.

The invigilator at your examination centre will explain the procedures to be followed for printing in that centre.

ACCENTS AND SPECIAL CHARACTERS

Find out if your program (and printer) can reproduce accents. Use this facility if it is available. If not write neatly in black pen.

At the end of Unit 4, you will have:

a revised all the text-processing theory which you learnt in Units 1, 2 and 3

b revised all the word processing functions on your program which you learnt in Units 1, 2 and 3.

Exercise 4A

Key in this letter to Mrs U Adamson, Careers Teacher, Queen Anne's High School, Wellington Cr, BURNDALE, BE2 5AB. Use a ragged right margin and mark URGENT. Save and print one copy. File name: EX4A. Use a Burndale letterhead.

Dear Mrs A____

VISITORS DAY ← lower case, initial caps & underscore

I am writing to tell you about next weeks Visitors Day at our College. Altho' it is rather short notice, I hope you will be able to attend, along w members of yr staff & pupils. I must apologise for the letters lateness; this is due to the fact that we have been waiting for the ~~printing~~ arrival of our brochure and application forms, to be completed. (, copies enclosed,)

We bel. ~~it~~ the V— D— is an excellent opp for school pupils to get the info they require and to exp a day in the working life of the College. Pupils can view the accom & rec (advice) & (help) in selecting a course to suit them. The College Admissions Dept wl be available to make sep appts for those ~~students~~ pupils who wishes to make a def commitment to a f/t course.

The College wl be open ~~from~~ between the hrs of 9 am + 1900 hrs on Thurs (next Thurs date) & a buffet lunch ~~is~~ wl be served in the ____________ for a limited number of careers ~~officers~~ teachers. I am sending a copy of this letter to the Head of yr 6th Form. Please return the enclosed form if you wish to join us for lunch – or telephone my sec on Ext 3164 asap.

Indent 1st para by ½" at left

Yrs scly

M/J CRABTREE
Marketing Officer, B— Tertiary College

LUNCH WILL BE IN TRAINING RESTAURANT

Exercise 4B

Please key in using a ragged right margin. Save as ~~[illegible]~~ EX4B and print one copy. Standardise layout of headings to lower case with underscore.

BURNDALE TERTIARY COLLEGE
Shaftesbury Road
BURNDALE BE1 3WB
} centre

BUSINESS ADMINISTRATION — centre & spaced caps

Full-time Courses [Bus Admin courses ~~are related to~~ follow National Vocational Qualifications (NVQs) ⁁at levels 2, 3 & 4. Students ~~study~~ a programme ~~course~~ based on there previous exp & qualifications, and designed to meet ~~their~~ each individuals needs. All courses run for 1 year but may be extended to two years for those who wish to improve their (qualifications) and (job prospects).

— double spacing

THE BUS ADMIN PROGRAMME
The ~~basic~~ core subjects are:

Typewriting
Word Processing
Computer Applications

⁁The timetable is organized in such a way that students can then ~~add~~ choose additional ~~options~~ (choices) from the the ✓ following list:

Shorthand
Audio-typewriting
Desk Top Publishing
German for Business*
Book-keeping
European Studies
French for Business*
Statistics for Business*

* A GCSE grade A-C ⁁in the relevant language is necessary in order to begin studying languages for business, and ⁁in mathematics for statistics for bus.

Our courses provide an excellent starting point for a career in the bus world. The skills learned can be transferred to many different jobs at different levels — from office junior to managing director.

The Admissions Officer is Jenny McEwan

Exercise 4B (continued)

Practical Experience

The majority of the work are practical in nature & students work at their own pace. Work placements are a valuable part of all are courses. Students work in local businesses for three weeks – one week ~~each~~ per term in a 3-term coarse.

HOW TO APPLY

An application form may be ~~filled~~ completed at any time – not just during the Spring and Summer terms. It can be a def advantage to apply early as the courses are popular. Forms shd be recd by the Admissions officer, —— ——, by the end of June so that preliminary interviews can be organised. However, late applications are very ~~useful~~ welcome. Its never to late!

COMMENCEMENT OF COURSES The courses wl begin on Mon 9 Sept at 9am. ~~Attendance~~ Lessons is from 0900 hrs to 5pm each day except Wednesday when the afternoon are left free for leisure/creative pursuits.

~~VISIT~~ COME TO OUR ~~OPEN~~ VISITORS DAY

Thurs (insert date)

0900- 1900 hrs

— centre

Exercise 4C

Retrieve file **EX4B**. Follow all the instructions shown below. Use double-line spacing unless it is specified otherwise. Save and print a copy of your work – use the filename **EX4C**.

BURNDALE TERTIARY COLLEGE
Shaftesbury Road
BURNDALE BE1 3WB
} single spacing

COURSES IN ⁄ B U S I N E S S   A D M I N I S T R A T I O N ← closed caps & underline

Full-time Courses

Business Administration courses are ~~related to~~ centred around National Vocational Qualifications (NVQs) at levels ~~II~~ 2, ~~III~~ 3 and ~~IV~~ 4. Students follow a ⁄ 'modular' programme ⁄ the structure of which is based on their previous experience and qualifications. ~~and designed to meet each individual's needs.~~ All courses run for 1 year ⁄ from Sep-June but may be extended to 2 years for those who wish to improve their job prospects ⁄ ~~and~~ & advanced qualifications.

Our courses provide an excellent ~~starting point~~ basis for a career in the business world. The skills learned can be transferred to many different jobs at different levels - from Office Junior to Managing Director.

(A)

CHANGE ALL SHOULDER HEADINGS TO CAPS AND REMOVE UNDERLINE

Operator:-
use the header (at top left of every page): BA/COURSES
use a footer (at bottom centre of every page) to number the pages in the format of: PAGE NO 1, PAGE NO 2...
starting on page 2
Keep the page breaks as indicated in the draft

Exercise 4C (continued)

The Business Administration Programme

The core subjects are:

Inset 1" from left margin

Typewriting
Word Processing
Computer Applications → Office Administration

The timetable is organized in such a way that students can then choose additional options from the following list:

Inset 1" from left margin

Shorthand	Book-keeping
Audio-typewriting	European Studies
German for Business*	French for Business*
Desk Top Publishing	Statistics for Business*

* A GCSE grade A-C in ~~the relevant language~~ German or French is necessary in order to begin studying languages for business, and in mathematics for 'Statistics for Business'.

(shorten line length of this para to 50)

Practical Experience

The majority of the ~~work~~ training is practical in nature and students work at their own pace. Work ~~placements are~~ exp is a valuable part of all our courses. Students carry out "real work" in local businesses for 3 weeks - 1 week per term in a 3-term course.

In the past, we have (wherever poss) organized a different work placement for each of the three weeks.

The College is proud of it's tecnology, eg 3 rooms of new up-to-date computers, two colour laser printers and a range of ~~industry~~ industry-standard softwear packages.

Use SINGLE LINE SPACING for inset sections and for the paragraph with line length shortened to 50

Exercise 4C (continued)

please change the word organized to organised throughout

(B)

How to Apply

Application forms for f/t courses

An application form may be completed at any time ~~- not just during the Spring and Summer terms~~. It can be a definite advantage to apply early as the courses are popular. ~~Forms~~ should be received by the Admissions Officer, Jenny McEwan, by the end of June so that preliminary interviews can be organized. However, late applications are very welcome. It's never too late!

Commencement of Courses

All f/t ~~The~~ courses commence ~~will begin~~ on Monday 9 September at 9.00 am. ~~Attendance is from 9.00 am to 5.00 pm each day except Wednesday when the afternoon is left free for leisure/creative pursuits.~~ // Enrolment dates for p/t courses are available from the College Reception & are also ~~published~~ 2 weeks prior to commencement in the local press.

Move this section to (B)

LEAVE 11 CLEAR LINES

COME TO OUR VISITORS DAY

Thursday (correct date inserted)

9.00 am - 7.00 pm

Copy to (A)

PART TIME COURSES

We offer a ~~full~~ wide range of part time courses either in single subjects (eg typewriting, word processing, shorthand) and also in B____ A____ NVQ Levels ~~3~~ 2 and 3. Some examples of this are listed below:

insert this section as Page 3

LEAVE REST OF PAGE BLANK FOR A LIST TO BE PHOTOCOPIED ONTO PAGE LATER

At the end of Unit 5, you will have learnt how to:

- **a** design the layout of a form using given headings/items
- **b** use different methods to allocate space on a form
- **c** use different methods of display.

You will already know how to complete a simple form with given information using preset enter points. In this unit you are going to carry out the actual design of the form itself using given headings/items.

General hints

Include all headings/items given in the draft and arrange these in a logical manner – use your initiative for the layout and plan it out on a piece of scrap paper first.

Allow suitable space after each heading/item displayed so that there is sufficient room for the relevant information to be inserted later. For example, you would need to allow more space for information on an address than you would for a date of birth.

Some headings may require two blocks of space to be made, for example:

Preferred destination: Choice 1 .... Choice 2 ....

(See also the section, 'Methods of space allocation' below.)

Decide whether the information which is to be inserted later (by the user of the form) will be carried out by hand, on a typewriter or on a word processor. This will often determine the method of layout, i.e., should the allocated space take the form of dotted lines or enter points?

Follow carefully the instructions in the draft for allocating space of specified size (*vertically and horizontally*) for illustrations/photographs, etc. Always use a ruler afterwards to check the print-out to make sure your settings are correct.

Give prominence to (*highlight*) specified headings/items in the form – see the section on methods of display below.

Make good use of the paper size (i.e., don't squash everything together!) – the end result should look clear and presentable.

Your word processing program may offer you many advanced form-design techniques to produce special effects such as line drawing, shaded boxes, etc. However, while often desirable in a business environment, these features are *not essential* requirements for the RSA III Part 2 examination. It would be unwise for examination candidates to spend too much time on producing unnecessary special effects for the form-design task at the expense of completing successfully the table and mail-merge tasks.

For examination purposes, therefore, complete the form-design task using the simplest and quickest methods; only use special effects *after* you have completed all the other examination tasks.

Methods of space allocation

Dotted lines: When leaving rows of dotted lines, remember to leave one space before the first dot. It is usually good practice to end all the dotted lines at the same position.

You should also use double-line spacing (or more) to allow sufficient room for the information to be inserted. For example:

Surname ....

First Name ....

Age .... Date of Birth ....

Enter points: Choose a suitable symbol for the enter points which does not normally appear in the text, e.g., a * or $.This will enable the operator who will complete the form later (by using the search facility to locate the enter points and replace them with the appropriate information) to do so with greater ease.
For example:

Surname $

First Name $

Age $ Date of Birth $

ALLOCATE SPACE

To allocate vertical space: 6 clear lines = 1 inch (25 mm)

To allocate horizontal space: 10 characters = 1 inch (25 mm) in 10-pitch
12 characters = 1 inch (25 mm) in 12-pitch

Methods of display/giving prominence

Sentences or paragraphs may be emphasized by changing the line spacing or insetting from the main margin (you should inset by at least 1 inch/25 mm).

As well as using bold, underline, capitals or spaced capitals to highlight headings or items, your program may allow you to choose other methods of displaying text, such as changing the font to italics, shadow, reverse image, larger size, etc.

The type of printer you are using will determine which methods of display can be supported, as some printers are not always capable of utilizing some advanced display features. Check with your tutor or printer manual and/or print a draft test copy to try out different effects.

FONT (to change size or appearance)

However, remember the caution at the beginning of this unit – only use special effects in an examination when you are absolutely sure you have enough time to complete all other tasks successfully!

Exercise 5A

5.1 Starting a new document, key in your name and the task number on Line 1. Design and prepare the membership form below leaving adequate amounts of space for insertions at the enter points (*).

Change the word **Disco** to **Dance** wherever it occurs in this task.

Save and print a copy of your work – use the filename **EX5A**.

Junior MEMBERSHIP FORM ← (spaced caps & centre)
Jo-Jo Junior Disco Team

Surname *
First Name *
Age *
Date of Birth *
Sex *

(also include the headings, Address, Tel No and Membership No)

(leave space here 2" across by 1½" down (51mm × 38mm) for a photograph)

Attending: JAZZ – Monday
MODERN DISCO – Wed
BALLET – Friday
CREATIVE DISCO – Sat
(please tick sessions to be attended)

Fee Paid *
Date of Joining *

(OPERATOR give prominence to the Attending: section)

Exercise 5B

5.2 Starting a new document, key in your name and the task number on Line 1. Design and prepare a telephone message form. The form will be completed by hand.

Save and print a copy of your work – use the filename **EX5B**.

Include the following headings where appropriate and leave suitable space for each item:

MESSAGE FOR, DATE, TIME,
CALLER'S NAME, CALLER'S COMPANY,
CALLERS TEL NO

TELEPHONE MESSAGE ← centre + underline

ACTION: URGENT / NON URGENT
RING BACK
WILL CALL AGAIN LATER

leave a space 2" across by 1" down (51mm x 25mm) for company name and stamp

MESSAGE ________________________

____

____

____

____

Received by __________ Date __________

give prominence to the ACTION section

Progress review checklist

Unit no.	Topic	Date completed	No. of errors
1	Use apostrophes correctly		
	Identify and correct errors of agreement, typographical and spelling errors		
	Produce a business letter on pre-printed letterhead		
	Change pitch for a document		
2	Complete reports and articles incorporating advanced text-processing features		
3	Use automatic page numbering with text		
	Use 'quick' copy/delete/move commands		
	Complete a multi-page document using advanced features		
4	Complete Consolidation 1 exercises as revision of theory and practice		
5	Design the layout of a form using given headings/items		
	Use different methods to allocate space on a form		
	Use different methods of display		
6	Enter footnotes using superscripted numbers		
	Rearrange table items in a specified order		
	Adapt a table to fit on the specified paper size		
	Change the pitch		
	Work out tab settings for an advanced table display		
	Use subdivided and multi-line column headings		
	Enter vertical column headings		
	Produce a table with ruled lines		
7	Create a mail-merge datafile		
	Create a mail-merge standard letter		
	Select records from a datafile		
	Merge and print a datafile with standard letter		
	Print a datafile		
	Print one page of a multi-page document		
8	Complete Consolidation 2 exercises as revision of theory and practice		

VAT No 354 6632 76

GEORGE CARTER & SON
125 Seaview Road
HORNSEA HN3 5PK

Tel No 0924-447825   Fax No 0924-552389

Accents (foreign words)

Allocate space

In single-line spacing: 6 clear lines = 1 inch.

(Remember to turn up an extra line space to leave a given measurement clear.)

10 characters = 1 inch (10 pitch)

12 characters = 1 inch (12 pitch)

Note: Remember to change right margin to allocate space at right of document

Automatic date format

Blocked capitals

Press: Caps lock key

Case – to switch

Centre text

To centre text before keying in:

To centre text already keyed in:

To remove centring:

Change logged disk drive to A

Clear the screen

Copy block of text

Create a new document

Cursor movement

Move cursor to required position	Use the arrow keys (cursor keys) → ← ↓↑ to move cursor to required position.
Move to start/end of document	**Press:** Home Home ↑ or Home Home ↓
Move left/right word by word	**Press:** Ctrl + ← or Ctrl + →
Move to start/end of line	**Press:** Home + ← or Home + →
Move to start/end of screen	**Press:** Home ↑ or Home ↓
Move cursor to specified page	**Press:** Ctrl + Home **Type:** No of page required ↵

Deleting text

Delete a character	Move cursor to incorrect character. **Press:** Del *or* Move cursor to right of incorrect character. **Press:** ← (Del)
Delete to end of line	
Delete to end of page	
Delete to end of sentence	
Delete a word	
Delete word left of cursor	
Delete word right of cursor	
Delete a block of text	

Edit text – delete and insert

Delete character(s)

Move cursor to incorrect character.
Press: Del (delete key) *or*

Move cursor to right of incorrect character.
Press: ⟵ Del (backspace delete key)

Delete a word

Replace text by overtyping (typeover)

Move cursor to incorrect entry.
Press: Ins key (typeover on)
Overtype with correct entry.
Press: Ins key (typeover off)

Insert characters or words

Position cursor where missing characters should be inserted:
Key in the missing character(s) or word(s)
Existing text will 'move over' to make room for the new text.

Embolden text

To embolden text before keying in:

To embolden text already keyed in:

To remove bold:

Enter points

To set up:

To search for:

(Use typeover mode if there is more that one enter point on the line. Remember to align enter points with a tab setting for information going on to more than one line.)

Exit the program

Flush right text

Font (to change size or appearance)

To change to a different font:

To change back to normal font:

To change font of text already keyed in:

Footers

To set a footer:

Footer with automatic page numbering:

Footnotes

Manual method

To enter footnote in body of text (no space before symbol):

Use asterisk(s) e.g., * ** ***
Or superscripted number(s) e.g., [3]
Leave one space after explanatory footnote symbol(s) at bottom of passage/document

Automatic method

To edit the footnote:

To delete the footnote:

To move the footnote:

Headers

Help function

Indent function

To indent at left margin:

To indent at left and right margin:

Insert text

Simply key in the missing character(s) at the appropriate place – the existing text will 'move over' to make room for the new text.

Justified right margin

Line draw (if available)

Line length – to change to fixed length

You can fit 82 characters across A4 paper using 10 pitch. If the left and right margins are set to 1 inch, then there are 62 characters across the typing line.
To reduce this to a 'fixed' length:

1. add all the required characters to left margin
2. add all the required characters to right margin
3. add some of required characters to left margin and some to right.

Line spacing

Mail merge

(Use a supplementary sheet if necessary.)

Margins (to change)

Move block of text

New page marker

Page numbering

To set page numbering:

Suppress page numbering on current page:

Paragraphs – splitting/joining

Make a new paragraph (i.e., split an existing paragraph into two)	Move cursor to first letter of new paragraph. **Press:** ↵ twice
Join two consecutive paragraphs into one	Move cursor to first character of second paragraph. **Press:** ← Del twice (backspace delete key) **Press:** Spacebar (to insert space(s)) after full stop

Pitch (to change)

Preview document

Print out

Check that the printer is switched on, is 'on-line' and has paper in it.

Quick copy/delete/move

Ragged right margin

Remove text emphasis

Replace text – typeover

Move cursor to incorrect entry. **Press**: Ins key (typeover on). Overtype with correct entry. **Press:** Ins key (typeover off).

Restore deleted text

Retrieve file

Ruled lines

Use underscore for horizontal lines and rule vertical lines in black pen, *or*

Save work to disk

Search for text

Search and replace text globally

Shade a block of text

Sort, by line

To sort items by line:

To sort, in descending order:

Spaced capitals

Press: Caps lock key
Leave one space after each letter.
Leave three spaces after each word.

Spellcheck

Standard paragraphs

Superscript

Switch on and load WP program

Table facility (if available)

(Use a supplementary sheet if necessary.)

Tabulation

Set a new tab:

Left-aligned tab:

Right-aligned tab:

Decimal tab:

Delete an individual tab setting:

Change the position of a tab setting:

Delete all tab settings together:

Reset tabs at regular settings:

Underline text

To underline text before keying in:

To underline text already keyed in:

To remove underline:

Vertical headings

Enter the heading one character per line, e.g.: D
O
W
N

View document

View file directory

Widow/orphan protection

OPPORTUNITIES UNLIMITED

West End Business Park
BOROUGHTON
BR4 7RF

Tel No: (0537) 544432 Fax No (0537) 68754 VAT No 184 9956 32

BURNDALE TERTIARY COLLEGE
Shaftesbury Road
BURNDALE
BE1 3WB

TEL NO (055) 375896
FAX NO (055) 623569

At the end of Unit 6, you will have learnt how to:

- **a** enter footnotes using superscripted numbers
- **b** rearrange table items in a specified order
- **c** adapt a table to fit on the specified paper size
- **d** change the pitch size
- **e** work out tab settings for an advanced table display
- **f** produce a table with ruled lines.

In the RSA Stage III Part 3 examination, the table task contains a number of additional features to the tabulation work you completed at Stage II.

If your program has a table facility, you will find this useful and quick to use after practice. Such facilities produce excellent tables quickly. Check with your tutor or manual before starting to key in Exercise 6B.

If your program does not have a table facility, you should refresh your memory on editing and tabulation procedures, methods of reducing the pitch size, altering margin settings, wrapping text on to next column, explanation of footnotes and rearranging the table items. The instructions for completing a table at Stage II level were given in *Extending Word Processing*. Additional instructions for more advanced techniques required for the table at Stage III are given in this unit.

Footnotes with superscripted numbers

A footnote is a piece of information placed at the end of each page (or document) which explains, in more depth, a particular point made within the body of the text.

A footnote symbol, such as a * or a superscripted number (e.g.,^{1}), is placed in the body of the text next to the word or phrase which needs further explanation. The same symbol is repeated at the end of the page or document with the explanatory text.

A 'superscripted' character is printed slightly above the standard line, e.g., 8.5^{2}.

There is *no space before* the footnote symbol in the body of the text. There is at least *one space between* the footnote symbol and the explanatory text at the end of the page/document.

To enter a footnote in superscript

- Position the cursor immediately after the word/character requiring a footnote.
- Change the font to superscript.
- **Key in** the footnote number – remember, there is *no space before* a footnote in the body of the text.
- Revert to normal text.

SUPERSCRIPT

The footnote number at the bottom of the page/document, with the explanatory text next to it, does *not* need to be in superscript.

FOOTNOTES

You can move, copy or delete a footnote in the same way that you would normally carry out these commands. Some programs have more sophisticated methods of footnote entry – check with your tutor or manual for instructions.

Exercise 6A

6.1 Starting a new document, key in your name and the task number on Line 1. Before going on to the table, let's practise inserting footnotes using superscripted numbers. Key in the following passage:

The Huns were a nomad people once scattered widely in Asia in the steppe country, north of the Caspian Sea. They were short in stature with black hair, yellow skins, broad noses and deep-set eyes. They settled, in the 5th century, north of the Danube in the lands which are now Austria and Hungary, and dominated the peoples who were led by Attila for some time.

6.2 Position the cursor immediately after the **s** of **Huns** in the first line of the passage above

Enter: [1] (in superscript)

6.3 Position the cursor immediately after the **y** of **Hungary**

Enter: [2] (in superscript)

6.4 Leave at least one clear line after the paragraph and enter the footnote explanation for footnote 1 as shown below (remember, you don't have to superscript the footnote in the explanation):

1 **The word 'Hun' has no reference to the German descent but denotes ferocity and destructiveness.**

6.5 Leave one clear line and enter the footnote explanation for footnote 2:

2 **In spite of their name, the Hungarians have no connection with the Huns.**

6.5 Print a copy of your work and check that your footnotes are correctly placed and in superscript as below:

The Huns[1] were a nomad people once scattered widely in Asia in the steppe country, north of the Caspian Sea. They were short in stature with black hair, yellow skins, broad noses and deep-set eyes. They settled, in the 5th century, north of the Danube in the lands which are now Austria and Hungary[2], and dominated the peoples who were led by Attila for some time.

1 **The word 'Hun' has no reference to the German descent, but denotes ferocity and destructiveness.**

2 **In spite of their name, the Hungarians have no connection with the Huns.**

Changing the pitch size

PITCH (to change)

If you have a lot of information to fit on the page, you may need to change the size of the pitch as you did for the letter in Unit 1. Word processors usually use 10-pitch (10 CPI – characters per inch) by default. However, most programs will allow you to select a smaller pitch size such as 12-pitch (12 CPI) – this will enable you to fit more data on to the table.

Your table should either be all in 10-pitch or all in 12-pitch – not a mixture!

Rearranging the table items

In the RSA Stage III examination, you will be asked to rearrange or sort the table into a particular order. There are several ways to do this. The choice is yours.

Method 1: Before you begin to key in the table, use a piece of scrap paper to note down, in advance, the order in which the entries should be keyed in. (It is better not to write on the exam paper itself as it may cause confusion.)

Method 2: Key in the entries as they are displayed, then use block and move functions to rearrange the items in the required order.

SORT, BY LINE

Method 3: Key in the entries as they are displayed, then if your program has a line-sort facility, use this to sort the items into the required order. To use line sort, the data must usually be set out in rows and columns. You can choose to sort alphabetically (A – Z) , or numerically (0, 1, 2, 3, 4 …). Therefore, line sort is only effective if each of the entries on the table takes up *one* line only, otherwise secondary lines will be included in the sort. (*Note:* Not all word processing programs offer this facility.)

Table – advanced features

In addition to normal editing and tabulation procedures, you may also be required to:

- include at least two footnotes in the form of superscripted numbers
- divide the columns of the table by a ruled line horizontally or vertically as specified
- enter horizontal and/or vertical column headings
- modify the layout as instructed
- rule the table (either by hand and/or on machine).

Ruled lines

There are several ways of ruling lines on to the table. Some programs have a special table facility, others have line-drawing facilities – they can even be put on by hand in black pen!

TABLE FACILITY (if available)

One of the simplest methods is to enter a line of underscores for the horizontal lines and rule in the vertical lines after printing by hand using a fine, clean, black pen and a 30 cm ruler with a smooth edge.

LINE DRAW (if available)

Extreme care should be taken to ensure that the lines are drawn neatly and accurately – no smudges, gaps where lines should join or missed lines! Take care, also, not to extend the line beyond its correct position, particularly where the lines meet at a corner. In the examination, every incorrect line is penalized!

RULED LINES

Remember to include enough space for the ruled lines when working out your tab settings.

Vertical column headings

Vertical column headings are relatively simple to enter using a word processor. The heading takes up one character per line which is read downwards instead of across. Set a tab stop in the normal way to position the vertical heading. The number of characters in the heading will determine the length of the vertical column heading area. For example:

ITEM DESCRIPTION	P A G E
Dungarees	4
Jumpers	6
Skirts	2

VERTICAL HEADINGS

Exercise 6B

6.7 Starting a new document, key in your name and the task number on Line 1. Set left and right margins at 1 inch. Work from the layout for the table, Exercise 6B. (Use your program's table facility if available.) Enter the footnotes as shown on the layout.

If you are using underscore or line draw for the horizontal lines when entering tab settings, note that you will also need to set a tab for the first column (**CAT REF NO**) at **12** to allow for the vertical line to be placed at the left margin at **10**. Therefore, set tabs for the column headings at: **12**, **18**, **37**, **50**, **68**.

After entering the column headings, delete the tab settings at **50** and **59** and replace with **decimal** tab settings at **53** and **62**.

Enter the horizontal and vertical lines using the most appropriate method described previously – it is largely up to the individual to try these out and adopt the method he or she can comfortably complete within the time limit of the Stage III examination.

Save and print a copy of your work – use the filename **EX6B**.

NEW RANGE OF DEVANE PRODUCTS

ADDITIONS TO THE CATALOGUE

CAT REF NO	STOCK DESCRIPTION	SIZE	COST[1]		PAGE
			-10	10+	
QW7	Devane Executive Case	18x13x5 in	£49.99	£45.99	5
QW3	Devane Leather Briefcase	18x13x5 in	£39.99	£35.99	2
QW8	Devane Attache Case	18x13x4 in	£59.99	£53.99	6
QW5	Devane Writing Case[2]	8x7x1 in	£17.99	£16.99	3

1 Bulk orders of 50+ qualify for a further discount.

2 Available in black, red or green.

6.8 Sort the table in order of **CAT REF NO**.

Save and print a copy of your work – use the same filename **EX6B**.

Exercise 6C

6.9 Starting a new document, key in your name and the task number on Line 1. Enter the table shown below. The items should be rearranged in ascending order of *start time* for each arena number (follow the layout of the first three items) – but keep the Junior and Adult sections separate as displayed. Rule as shown.

You may need to change the font to 12-pitch so the table will fit on A4 paper with the shorter edge at the top, without changing the margins. If the table still won't fit the page, reduce the margins to $^1/_2$ inch.

Save and print a copy of your work – use the filename **EX6C**.

SILSTON SUMMER FESTIVAL ← centre

EVENT TIME		DISPLAY TEAM	EVENT NAME	NAME OF ORGANISER	ARENA
START	END				
Junior Section					
1400	1430	JAY DANCEBIRDS	Sun & Wind[1]	June Berry	1
1435	1500	FARRAH SINGERS	Junior Medley	Ann Shaw	1
1505	1525	JAY DANCEBIRDS	Dreams & Destinies	June Berry	1
1455	1525	FARRAH SINGERS	Southern Belle	Ann Shaw	~~2~~ 3
1505	1525	DANCE MINORS	Sugar and Spice	Maria Lee	2
1400	1500	FARRAH GYM SQUAD	Gymnastics	Mark Drew	2
1400	1445	SILSTON CHOIR	Yankee Doodle Dandy	Alan Green	3
Adult Section					
1530	1630	LAVELL DANCERS	Jazz American	Sue Vine	1
1645	1745	SILSTON Band	Bonanza Brass	Paul Knell	2
1630	1530	SILSTON BAND	City Lights	Paul Knell	3
1610	1630	THE DEVETTES	Guitar Duette[2]	Jo Devette	2
1645	1745	SILSTON CHOIRE	Showboat ~~Time~~	Alan Green	3
~~1530~~	~~1600~~	~~DANCE MAJORS~~	~~World Dance~~	~~Maria Lee~~	~~2~~
1530	1600	FARRAH SINGERS	ADULT Medley ~~Hawaii~~	Ann Shaw	2
1645	1745	SILSTON CHOIR	~~Capacabana~~	Alan Green	1

1 A mixture of classical ballet, jazz over the last century (and contemporary dance music)

2 Speciality act featuring Spanish Flamenco guitar & Spanish dancing by the Jay Dancebirds

please emphasise the words "Junior Section" and "Adult Section"

At the end of Unit 7, you will have learnt how to:

- **a** create a mail-merge datafile on your program
- **b** create a mail-merge standard letter on your program
- **c** select records from your datafile, using one or more criteria
- **d** merge and print the datafile with the standard letter
- **e** print one page of a multi-page document.

Mail merge (or mail shot)

Mail merge is the combining (merging) of data from two files into one file. The most common use of this feature is the production of 'personalized' letters. (An unpopular example of this is 'junk mail' – the same letter is sent out to many people, but printed with the individual's own name and address and other personal details.)

One file is the standard letter which is to be sent to many different addresses. Another file is the datafile containing the different names and addresses (and sometimes other relevant data).

In the RSA Stage III Part 2 examination, you are required to key in:

- **a** a standard letter
- **b** a datafile of 10 addresses.

You will then select a particular cross-section (usually six) of the addressees to receive the letter.

Finally, you will 'merge' the standard letter with the selected addressees from the datafile and then print the letters. (*Note*: You are also required to produce print-outs of the standard letter and the full datafile.)

Creating your datafile

The method varies from one program to another, although the principle is the same. Check with your manual and your tutor throughout the mail-merge unit. The order of working within you program may be different from that given in this unit.

Each addressee will have a 'record' keyed in for them. Each record is made up of separate 'fields'. Look at the example below showing Mrs Waterston's record:

`Mrs P Waterston`
`12 Oak Drive`
`Netherton`
`EDGERTON`
`EN5 9OL`
		Name and Address Field

`Mrs Waterston`	–	Salutation Field
`Veteran`	–	Variable Data Field

As you enter each *record* into the datafile, you will insert a code for each *field*. The same codes will be used in the standard letter. The program will insert the relevant information from the datafile at the points where the codes have been placed in the letter.

You may wish to name the fields as Field 1, Field 2, Field 3. Each record should contain *the same number of fields* and the fields should appear in *the same order in each record*.

MAIL MERGE (codes for datafile)

Each field should always contain *the same kind of information*: in the example above the salutation field must, of course, actually contain the name of the addressee in every record. (*Note*: It is important that other text, such as your name, is *not* included in the datafile. If you do this, the mail merge may not 'run'. You can *write* your name on your datafile *after* it is printed *or* you can retrieve your datafile, key in your name and print *after the mail merge has been run and printed*.)

Exercise 7A

7.1 Create your datafile. Starting a new document, key in the following name and address. Insert a merge code for the name and address field (or Field 1):

```
Mrs P Waterston
12 Oak Drive
Netherton
EDGERTON
EN5 9OL
```

7.2 Key in **Mrs Waterston**. Insert a merge code for the salutation field (or Field 2).

7.3 Key in **Veteran**. Insert a merge code for the variable data field (or Field 3).

7.4 If necessary within your progam, insert a code to indicate the end of the first record.

7.5 Key in the following four records to complete your datafile. Insert merge codes for the three fields in the appropriate positions, along with any necessary 'end-of-record' codes.

Mr I K Thompson
26 Summer Close
Sunley
LANGTON
LN9 6EJ
Mr Thompson
Ordinary

Mr M E Willson
26 Fairway
ROYDEN
RN6 4JL
Mr Willson
Veteran

Mrs M Horsfall
18 Lea Rd
Leafield
BROOK HILL
BK7 2HK
Mrs Horsfall
Veteran

Ms V Varley
4 Water Lane
NORFIELD
ND16 8LL
Ms Varley
Ordinary

7.6 Proofread and correct the records if necessary. Save your datafile as **DATA7A**. Clear your screen.

Printing your datafile

In the RSA Stage III Part 2 examination, you are asked to print a copy of the full datafile (usually 10 records). No more than two sheets of paper should be used from your examination allocation for this purpose.

In some programs, the datafile will automatically be printed on one or two sheets of paper but other programs will cause each record to be printed on a separate sheet, using up most of your allocated paper in the examination. Find out how your program will print the datafile:

- *If no more than two sheets of paper will be used,* print the datafile as soon as you have keyed it in and proofread it.
- *If your program prints each record on a separate sheet,* do not print your datafile until you have run and printed the mail merge task successfully. You can then retrieve the datafile and remove the 'end-of-record' or 'page break' codes before printing, or take any other necessary steps to ensure the datafile prints out on one or two pages only.

MAIL MERGE (datafile to print)

7.7 After reading the information on printing your datafile, print a copy of your datafile now *if relevant to your program.*

Standard letter

The standard letter will contain merge codes to show where variable information is to be inserted during the merging procedure. Look at the example below:

Date

[Name and address field (or Field 1)]

Dear [Salutation field (or Field 2)]

As a [Variable data field (or Field 3)] member of our Club, I am writing to ask you if you would like to attend our Annual Dinner to be held in two months' time. I attach full details and a tear-off slip.

Please return the completed slip as soon as possible to be sure of a reservation.

Yours sincerely

M R Cheeseman
Chairman

Enc

MAIL MERGE
(codes for standard letter)

When you key in the standard letter, you insert merge codes into the standard letter at the points where data will be extracted from the datafile, e.g., at [] above.

Exercise 7A (continued)

7.8 Create your standard letter. Starting with a clear screen, key in **your name** and **Exercise 7A** on Line 1.

7.9 Key in the standard letter shown below, inserting merge codes for Fields 1, 2 and 3 in the appropriate positions.

(Today's date)

[Merge code for Name and address field (Field 1)]

Dear [Merge code for Salutation field (Field 2)]

I am pleased to be able to tell you that the event which has been organised for our spring run is open to [Variable data field (Field 3)] members. Please contact me if you would like further details.

Yours sincerely

James Stevens
Events Organiser

7.10 Save your standard letter as **LETT7A** and clear the screen.

7.11 Print a copy of your standard letter.

Selecting the records to be merged

MAIL MERGE
(select records from datafile)

A datafile will often contain details of the full range of a company's clients or customers, or all of a club's members. However, a particular letter may need to be sent to only a selection of the customers or members. For example, in the small datafile which you have just keyed in, a letter may be sent to all the 'Ordinary' members or all the 'Veteran' members.

In the RSA Stage III Part 2 examination, you are asked to select a number of records from the datafile (usually 6 records from 10).

Exercise 7A (continued)

7.12 To select the required addressees from your datafile, follow the instructions relevant to your program to select all the records with the word **Veteran** as Field 3 in your datafile **DATA7A**.

7.13 Check that three records have been selected from the five which you inserted (for Mrs Horsfall, Mr Willson and Mrs Waterston).

7.14 Save your selected records as **SORT7A** and clear the screen.

Merging the datafile with the standard letter

MAIL MERGE
(merging files)

After preparing the standard letter, and selecting the appropriate records from the datafile, the two files are merged to produce letters which are 'personalized'.

In the RSA Stage III Part 2 examination, you are required to produce six merged letters by merging the *selected datafile* and the *standard letter*. To avoid confusion, always save your selected datafile of six records with a completely different name (e.g., SORT—) from the original datafile of 10 records (e.g., DATA—). Always save your six merged letters under a different name (e.g., MERGE —) from the original standard letter (e.g., LETT—).

Exercise 7A (continued)

7.15 To merge the selected records with the standard letter, merge the selected datafile (**SORT7A**) and the standard letter (**LETT7A**). Save the merged letters as **MERG7A**.

Printing mail merge documents

MAIL MERGE
(printing documents)

PRINT ONE PAGE OF
MULTI-PAGE DOCUMENT

In the RSA Stage III Part 2 examination, you are required to print six letters on plain paper after merging the *selected datafile* and the *standard letter*.

In the examination, you are required to print out all of the merged letters. However, while you are practising you might like to save paper by printing out only *one* letter for checking.

If you are working with a tutor, you could demonstrate that your mail merge has worked satisfactorily by having the file of six letters on screen.

7.16 Print **one** of your merged letters from file **MERG7A**. If necessary, clear your screen.

MAIL MERGE
(datafile to print)

7.17 *If you did not print your datafile at 7.6*, do so now, by retrieving the file **DATA7A** and ensuring that the data will be printed on no more than two sheets of paper.

Selecting records using more than one criterion

MAIL MERGE
(selecting on more than one criterion)

In the RSA Stage III Part 2 examination, and in practice, it may be necessary for you to sort the datafile using two 'keys'. For example, to select the three records with the criterion **4 April** from the list below, you may have to use the key **4** *and* the key **April**.

3 April	13 April	4 November
4 April	4 March	14 April
21 June	25 June	27 April
4 April	4 July	4 April

Find out how to sort on two criteria as above in your program. Your program may not require separate 'keys' to be inserted for each criterion.

Exercise 7B

7.18 Starting a new document, key in the following records as a datafile. Save as **DATA7B** and print one copy.

Mrs J Brookner
36 Windsor Rd
Wooldale
Huddersfield
HD7 8WB
Mrs Brookner
Jazz Adult

Ms L Knight
Thorn View
Kirkwood
Huddersfield
HD6 9DH
Ms Knight
Jazz Junior

Mr E Dale
125 Newton Hill
Brighouse
HD6 3ME
Mr Dale
Creative Junior

Mr B Brown
10 Sandy Hill Lane
Sowerby Bridge
HX3 3PO
Mr Brown
Jazz Junior

Mr O Kozlowski
147 Kirkstone Ave
Highley
Brighouse
HD6 2BE
Mr Kozlowski
Jazz Junior

Mr P M Robinson
151 Meadow Grove
Kirkwood
Huddersfield
HD6 4HM
Mr Robinson
Creative Adult

Ms R E Rose
14 Wykeham Rise
Keighley
BD22 5DD
Ms Rose
Creative Junior

Exercise 7B (continued)

7.19 Starting a new document, key in the letter.

This letter is to be sent to all our Jazz Junior members, telling them about the competition. Please use today's date, ragged right margin, and print the letters. Save your letter as LETT8B

*
*
*
* } address field

Dear * salutation field

NORTHERN /JAZZ DUO COMPETITION /JUNIOR

The annual competition wl take place / as usual at Milltown Civic ~~Centre~~ Hall on Sat 2 May.

For the past few years, we have ~~been~~ entered between 4 and six couples and, last yr, Gary Murphy & Anna Mayman / were winners in the Under-13 section. (of our Club)

As a regular attender at our * variable field sessions, I wd like to invite you to enter the competition and I enclose an application form. Please complete & return this to me asap giving the name of yr proposed partner. [Further (details) & (info) about our special competition training ~~classes~~ sessions can be obtained from Mary Steward.

Yrs scly

Michelle Woodman
MEMBERSHIP SEC

Enc

Exercise 7C

7.20 Starting a new document, key in the datafile.

Mrs C Beaty
16 Tennyson Drive
BACKWOOD
BD4 7MA
Cathy
Branch 1 Personnel

Mr A L Brearley
Bridge End
BROWNSHAW
BW9 3AB
Adrian
Branch 1 Personnel

Mrs W Cawdwell
10 Dean Cottages
Deanshaw
HIGH WELLS
HS3 3NB
Wendy
Branch 2 Personnel

Mr A K Basu
6 Hill View Drive
Carr Hill
BROWNSHAW
BW3 4HA
Asoke
Branch 1 Personnel

Ms A Forder
18 Thomas St
Southwood
BACKWOOD
BD6 7LJ
Alison
Branch 3 Personnel

Miss L Lord
10 Overwood Ln
Overwood
LONSDALE
LE9 6SN
Lynda
Branch 1 Personnel

Miss S Hussain
29 Nelson Ave
Renshaw
RAWTON
RN6 8JL
Shahena
Branch 1 Accounts

Miss J L Stocks
Birch View
BACKWOOD
BD10 4LM
Jenny
Branch 1 Personnel

Mrs C Lefevre
16 Lindon Way
RAWTON
RN5 7LM
Claire
Branch 1 Purchasing

Mr H Fischer
16 Trafford Close
Merevale
HIGH WELLS
HS4 9LW
Helmut
Branch 1 Personnel

Exercise 7C (continued)

7.21 Starting a new document, key in the letter to be sent to all *Branch 1 Personnel* staff. Use today's date and justified right margin. Change **Head of Department** to **Section Manager** throughout.

*
*
*
*
*

CAPS

Human Resource Management – Current Issues

Dear *

The Co is holding training ~~courses~~ sessions over the coming 6 months & I wd like to invite you to attend. I am writing to all staff employed in *. ~~departments throughout our organisation~~.

[The sessions wl run for 2 or 3 days, depending on the content, and accom wl be provided. The following ~~venues~~ towns wl (✓) be used:

BIRMINGHAM
LEEDS
GLASGOW
ABERDEEN
NEWCASTLE
BRISTOL
LONDON
BELFAST

Please leave space for logo at left – to measure at least 3" across x 2" down – (75mm x 50mm)

Attendance wl be at the discretion of yr Head of Dept with whom you shd discuss yr interest. I enclose full details of the various courses & an application form. Please return yr (form) (completed) to yr Head of Dept. [I look forward to seeing you at one of the above venues.

I hope you will ~~find~~ consider the proposed sessions ~~to be~~ relevant to yr day-to-day work. It is our policy to keep abreast of new developments in current ~~practise~~ practice & to apply new ideas in a practical way w the complete involvement of staff at all levels.

Yrs sincerely

PERFECT BUILDING SOCIETY

M D TRAVIS
Personnel Director

Encs

Printing-out arrangements in the RSA Stage III Part 2 examination

You are given 12 sheets of A4 paper in this examination.
This is sufficient to be able to print out the following:

- 1 *draft* copy of the table
- 1 *final* copy of the table
- 1 *final* copy of the form
- 1 *final* copy of your datafile (allowing two sheets)
- 1 *final* copy of your standard letter
- 6 *final* copies of the merged letters.

You *will not* have sufficient paper to print a draft copy of any of the tasks, except the table. Use the preview facility to make sure your documents are accurate before you save and print.

The printing of the final copies of the tasks in this examination is done outside the examination time of one and one-quarter hours *by the candidate*.
No amendments may be made to the text after that time has expired. You are allowed to insert special characters, such as accents, on to the final copies after the examination time.

If you have used a method of ruling the table which produces *only horizontal lines* on the printer, you will draw in the vertical lines with a pen after printing this task.

Don't forget that the mail-merge task requires you to print:

- the full datafile of 10 records
- the standard letter
- copies of the merged letter (usually six).

The invigilator at your examination centre will explain the procedures to be followed for printing in that centre.

Exercise 8A

Please prepare this application form. Include the following headings where appropriate and allow sufficient space for each item inserting a symbol such as a * or @ at infill points. Change the word **trip(s)** to **excursion(s)** wherever it occurs in this task and also in the next task, **Exercise 8B**.

Save and print a copy of your work – use the filename **EX8A**.

Surname, Forenames, Address, Date of Birth, Payroll No, Department, No of Adult Places Required, No of Child Places Required, Signed, Date

APPLICATION FORM ← spaced caps

Company Weekend Trip

leave a space here at least 2½" across by 2½" down (63 mm × 63mm) for a company logo

Trip A: PARIS ___

Trip B: AMSTERDAM ___

Trip C: VIENNA ___

(please tick choice required)

I apply for a total of ___ places for the above trip. I agree to abide by the company rules and regulations for the duration of the trip

put the section for "Trips" in bold

Exercise 8B

Prepare this table, using the paper with the shorter edge at the top. Rearrange the employee names in alphabetical order of *surname* within each section. Rule as shown.

Save and print a copy of your work – use the filename **EX8B**.

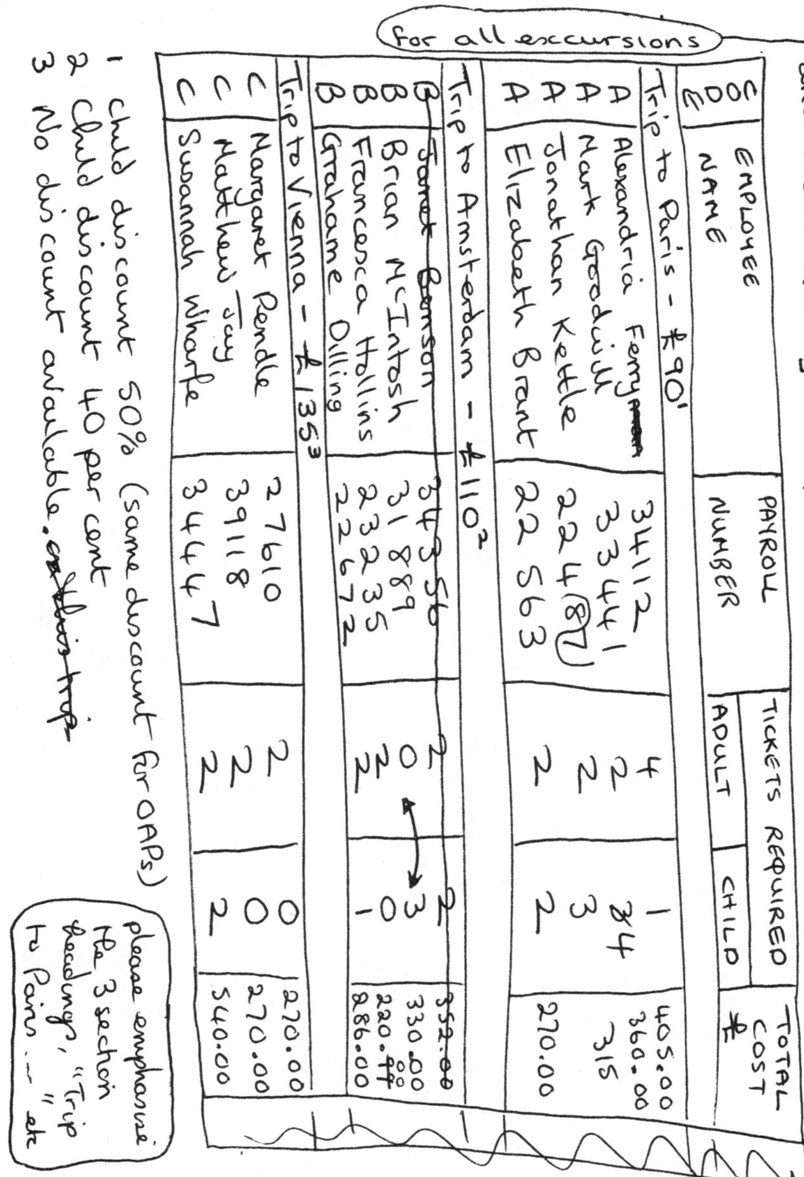

COMPANY WEEKEND TRIP ← (centre)

The following personnel are to be included on the 3 co weekend trips. Coaches will depart from Head Office on Friday 26 Sep at 1330 hrs, and ~~return~~ Monday 29 Sep at 2230 hrs

CODE	EMPLOYEE NAME	PAYROLL NUMBER	TICKETS REQUIRED		TOTAL COST
			ADULT	CHILD	£
Trip to Paris - £90[1]					
A	Alexandria Ferry	34112	4	1	405.00
A	Mark Goodwill	33441	2	~~3~~ 4	360.00
A	Jonathan Kettle	224(87)	2	3	315
A	Elizabeth Brant	22563	2	2	270.00
Trip to Amsterdam - £110[2]					
~~B~~	~~Janet Benson~~	~~34356~~	~~2~~	~~2~~	~~352.00~~
B	Brian McIntosh	31889	0 ↔	3	330.00
B	Francesca Hollins	23235	2	0	220.~~44~~ 00
B	Grahame Dilling	22672	2	1	286.00
Trip to Vienna - £135[3]					
C	Margaret Rendle	27610	2	0	270.00
C	Matthew Jay	39118	2	0	270.00
C	Susannah Wharfe	34447	2	2	540.00

(for all excursions)

1 child discount 50% (same discount for OAPs)
2 Child discount 40 per cent
3 No discount available. ~~on this trip~~

please emphasise the 3 section headings, "Trip to Paris ..." etc

Exercise 8C

(Please set up and print a data file with these 10 records)

Mrs P Grant
Grattan & Moore Ltd
12-15 Cornfield Street
BRADFORD
BD3 4NF
Mrs Grant
11 July-15 July

Miss K M Bolton
Birkby Signs Ltd
Birkby Lane West
CLECKHEATON
CN9 6BD
Miss Bolton
11 July-15 July

Mr M Akram
Greaves Bros Ltd
Slade Street
HALIFAX
HX2 3ES
Mr Akram
11 August-15 August

Ms Y Wigglesworth
Outwood Electrics Plc
Royd Mill
LIVERSEDGE
BD13 3RS
Ms Wigglesworth
11 July-15 July

Mr K Firth
Firth Kitchens Ltd
West Road Mill
HUDDERSFIELD
HD2 7SF
Mr Firth
11 July-15 July

Mrs J Baines
Vale Components PLC
Vale Hill
DEWSBURY
WF10 5MP
Mrs Baines
11 July-15 July

Mrs S Saddique
Long & James Ltd
16 Melbury Road
SOWERBY BRIDGE
HX3 1EL
Mrs Saddique
11 August-15 August

Mrs P A House
Newall Products Ltd
Paddock Ave
SKIPTON
BD30 4DD
Mrs House
11 July-15 July

Mr S E Pedlipska
Pedlipska Plant Hire Ltd
Hollinwell Works
KEIGHLEY
BD22 1HP
Mr Pedlipska
21 July-25 July

Mr M N Neocleous
Hellenic Foods
Valley Business Park
BRIGHOUSE
HD5 2AV
Mr Neocleous
21 August-25 August

Exercise 8C (continued)

Please send this letter to all the companies which are interested in the dates 11 July – 15 July. Use a ragged right margin.

*
*
*
*
*

Dear *

emphasise — Northern News Weekend Breaks

Thank you for contacting me about our new excursions programme. [I note that you wd be interested in arranging a ~~weekend~~ break in Amsterdam for employees at your Co for the ~~weekend~~ dates of *, and I have pleasure in enclosing full details.

The Hotel ~~Excellente~~ Parador wl be our base for the weekend. [As you can see from the photograph, it is a large, modern hotel w a wide range of amenities. (Colour leaflets enclosed.)

Allow a square here 2" x 2" (50mm x 50mm) for photo

The cost per person wl be £210 and this includes travel to and from ~~Bradford~~ Leeds, accom on a bed & breakfast basis, and insurance. Parties of 12 and over ~~attract the privel~~ privilege of one free place for the ~~organiser~~ leader.

Please ~~contact me by~~ telephone me asap if you wish to make a def reservation as demand is proving to be unexpectedly high.

Yours ffly
NORTHERN NEWS

M Hickson
Travel Manager
Encs

Unit 1

Apostrophes

You're late! We've been waiting for you. Sit down and we'll start or there'll be no food left for you.

Don't say you can't do the work. It's not difficult and there's no reason why you shouldn't finish it.

The sun's glare caused the player's eyes to lose sight of his opponent's ball. The game's end was announced and the winner's victory was acknowledged by the other team's captain.

The city's streets were crowded as tourists and residents waited to see the Mayor's car arrive at the Club's entrance. The Freedom of the City was to be bestowed on the city's football team and its manager.

It's your decision as to whether you wish to bring the dog on Saturday. It's well-behaved and the children like its friendly nature. They were pleased to hear that it's recovered from its recent illness and they are looking forward to its coming so that it can play with its new toys and they can see for themselves that it's fit and well again.

We were always told to be careful to dot our i's and cross our t's but the typewriter, which must date from the 1950's or 1960's, wouldn't print w's and p's and missed the tails off the y's, q's and g's.

Exercise 1A

OPPORTUNITIES UNLIMITED

West End Business Park
BOROUGHTON
BR4 7RF

Tel No: (0537) 544432 Fax No (0537) 68754 VAT No 184 9956 32

Date of typing Name Ex 1A

PRIVATE

Mrs A Bottomley
26 Hollings Way
BOROUGHTON
BB10 1WB

Dear Mrs Bottomley

<u>'GOING IT ALONE' SEMINAR - SATURDAY (correct date inserted for Saturday after next)</u>

Further to yesterday's telephone conversation, I would like to let you have more information on the above event which is aimed at providing prospective 'entrepreneurs' with the opportunity to acquire as much information as possible. At the seminar, you will be able to benefit from the knowledge and experience of local leaders of industry and business.

> At Opportunities Unlimited, we acknowledge the fact that setting up in business on your own is an enormous step to take and we aim to help the budding businessman or businesswoman through the early stages.

The day will begin at 9.30 am with a talk by our Director, followed by approximately one hour of presentations on current 'start-up' schemes. After coffee at 11.00 am, the participants will be invited to separate into small groups and to pool their ideas and experiences in considering what makes a successful business. The afternoon will be your chance to put your idea(s) to an advisor and to receive individual advice.

I enclose a map showing the location of our temporary accommodation, and a leaflet on the seminar. I have sent a copy of this letter to Ms P Farren, your colleague. I look forward to seeing you at the seminar.

Yours faithfully

E A Sutcliffe
Conference Organiser

Encs

Copy to Ms P Farren

Exercise 1B

VAT No 354 6632 76

GEORGE CARTER & SON
125 Seaview Road
HORNSEA HN3 5PK
Tel No 0924-447825 Fax No 0924-552389

Date of typing Name Ex1B

FOR THE ATTENTION OF THE HEALTH AND SAFETY OFFICER

Baxter, Green & Co
Yates Quay
EASTPORT
ET4 7GH

Dear Sirs

A GOOD PLACE TO WORK?

Thank you for contacting me recently in response to our newspaper advertisement.

The GOOD PLACE TO WORK? campaign began in (last month) of this year and has definitely received a good response, both from employers and employees. The project employs 3 full-time workers, and approximately 3 part-time assistants from the region are used at each venue to ensure information reaches local organisations.

Our campaign's mobile caravan will be in the Eastport area in (month after next) and, as you know, we are looking for a suitable site to locate the caravan. It is necessary for us to be in the business centre of a town with sufficient car parking space for people to be encouraged to visit the exhibition without inconvenience. Your SEAVIEW ROAD factory would appear to be ideal and I have written to your Managing Director, James Green, requesting permission to use your company's resources. I have sent him a copy of this letter.

I enclose a brochure giving information on the project and exhibition and hope to hear from you before (a week on Friday) so that arrangements can be finalised.

Yours faithfully

H HAMILTON
Project Leader

Enc

Copy to James Green, Managing Director, Baxter, Green & Co

Exercise 1C

VAT No 354 6632 76

GEORGE CARTER & SON
125 Seaview Road
HORNSEA HN3 5PK
Tel No 0924-447825 Fax No 0924-552389

Date of typing Name EX1C

FOR THE ATTENTION OF THE HEALTH AND SAFETY OFFICER

Baxter, Green & Co
Yates Quay
EASTPORT
ET4 7GH

Dear Sirs

A GOOD PLACE TO WORK?

Thank you for contacting me recently in response to our newspaper advertisement.

The GOOD PLACE TO WORK? campaign began in (last month) of this year and has definitely received a good response, both from employers and employees. The project employs 3 full-time workers, and approximately 3 part-time assistants from the region are used at each venue to ensure information reaches local organisations.

Our campaign's mobile caravan will be in the Eastport area in (month after next) and, as you know, we are looking for a suitable site to locate the caravan. It is necessary for us to be in the business centre of a town with sufficient car parking space for people to be encouraged to visit the exhibition without inconvenience. Your SEAVIEW ROAD factory would appear to be ideal and I have written to your Managing Director, James Green, requesting permission to use your company's resources. I have sent him a copy of this letter.

It is very important that as many people as possible visit the exhibition in view of the fact that legislation is already in place. The European Community guidelines set out clear responsibilities for employers and employees alike and all managers/supervisors need to be made aware of the part they must play in assessing workstations.

It is, of course, no less vital that work practices are also examined with the aim of increasing efficiency and decreasing potential dangers and factors which might promote disease and discomfort.

Exercise 1C (continued)

Name EX1C

We hope to dispel some myths by giving factual information and advice based on thorough research.

I enclose a brochure giving information on the project and exhibition and hope to hear from you before (a week on Friday) so that arrangements can be finalised.

Yours faithfully

H HAMILTON
Project Leader

Enc

Copy to James Green, Managing Director, Baxter, Green & Co

Exercise 2A

Name Exercise 2A

GOING IT ALONE SEMINAR

Saturday (correct date inserted)

Opportunities Unlimited are pleased to organise this Seminar for prospective business owners in the Boroughton area.

Our offices are to be relocated in the West End Business Park, where our new, purpose-built accommodation is nearing completion. In the meantime, we are fortunate that we have been allowed to use the premises of the Vendôme Hotel, High Street, for our Seminar.

The Seminar will be held in the ground floor function suite and the programme for the day has been organised as follows:

0900 HRS - INTRODUCTION

Neil Ross, Marketing Director of Opportunities Unlimited will outline the programme for the day and will introduce the speakers and representatives from local industry, business and commerce.

1000 HRS - START-UP SCHEMES

Presentations will be made by the High Street banks, the Small Business Advisory Service and the British Franchise Association.

Topics will include: capital, loans, share issues, government schemes and development boards.

1100 HRS - COFFEE

1115 HRS - WHAT MAKES AN ENTREPRENEUR?

With the aid of case histories, participants will be encouraged to discuss the viability of the respective businesses, types of business organisation, franchising, market research, and employment law. The leader of each group will advise on Income Tax, VAT and National Insurance. The aim is to make the participants more aware of the pitfalls and pleasures of self-employment.

Exercise 2A (continued)

Name Exercise 2A

<u>1245 HRS - LUNCH IN 1ST FLOOR CARVERY</u>

<u>1400 HRS - CONSULTATION SESSIONS</u>

The 'experts' will make themselves available for individual consultation. Every participant can put forward his or her idea and receive valuable assistance.

<u>1600 HRS - PLENARY SESSION/PRIZE PRESENTATION</u>

Neil Ross, Marketing Director, will present an award - 'Business Idea of the Day' - together with a cheque for £250 to the 'entrepreneur' with the most original (and viable) business proposal.

(The winner will be chosen by all the experts present at the Seminar.)

Exercise 2B

Name Exercise 2B

A G O O D P L A C E T O W O R K ?

<u>An Exhibition for Office Workers</u>

The Information Technology revolution has changed the way we work and brought many benefits - both from the employer's point of view and the employees' angle. Although there are no serious occupational dangers such as you might find in an engineering workshop or a foundry, the office does have its own risks.

<u>Managers/Supervisors</u> Do you know what your responsibilities are under EC legislation?

It will be your job to assess every workstation in your section/department. It's up to you to make sure EC recommendations are met.

<u>Electronic Office Workers/VDU Operators</u> Do you suffer from eye strain, aching shoulders, back pain, headaches? What can you do to make your working day more comfortable? How can your employer help?

VISIT THE GOOD PLACE TO WORK EXHIBITION

Help yourself to a better workplace

<u>The exhibition will offer</u>:

- Inter-active Video
- Slides
- Displays
- Professional Advice
- Quizzes, Questionnaires

Exercise 2B (continued)

Name   Exercise 2B

LEARN ABOUT 3 AREAS OF INTEREST

Health   Eye problems, muscular strain, repetitive strain injury, VDUs and problems with pregnancy. Is it really the computer's fault? What can be done to alleviate stress, strain and worry?

Ergonomics   Workstations, systems, the workplace environment. It's usually easy to change some aspects such as chairs, desks, and lighting but it's more difficult to change the way we think and work!

This is a very extensive topic - you'll be surprised what's involved.

Safety   Electricity, radiation, chemicals. Expediency can lead to inadequate and dangerous practices in the use of electricity. There are many toxic chemicals in offices (but there's no risk provided due care is taken). We'll give you the facts about radiation from VDUs.

Exhibition opens at 1000 hrs Monday - Saturday and closes at

1800 hrs Monday - Friday. (Early close Saturday 1600 hrs.)

Phone 071-124367 for exact location in your town - ask for

Hamish Hamilton.

A GOOD PLACE TO WORK?

APPEARING SOON IN A CAR PARK NEAR YOU!

Exercise 3A

Name   Exercise 3A   BUSINESS SEMINAR

G O I N G I T A L O N E S E M I N A R

Saturday (correct date inserted)

Opportunities Unlimited are pleased to organise this Seminar for

prospective business owners in the Boroughton area.

The Seminar is the first of its kind in the area and should

attract much publicity from the media. We are hoping to organise

suitable press coverage, eg the local newspapers.

The required fee for the full day

will be £75.00 including lunch.

The Seminar will be chaired by

Adam Flynn, Marketing Director of

Opportunities Unlimited.

REF: OU/SH

Exercise 3A (continued)

Name   Exercise 3A   BUSINESS SEMINAR

THE PROGRAMME FOR THE DAY HAS BEEN ORGANISED AS FOLLOWS:

0900 HRS - INTRODUCTION

Adam Flynn, Marketing Director of Opportunities Unlimited will outline the programme for the day. He will then introduce speakers and representatives from local industry, business and commerce including:

1	Mr Ahmed Khan	-	CHAIRMAN, Ridings & Holt Ltd
2	Mr Paul Knight	-	MANAGING DIRECTOR, Vernons & Hoyle Ltd
3	Mrs Vanessa Debarry	-	SOLICITOR, Mayes, Drew & Smithies
4	Ms Gladys Fairway	-	MANAGING DIRECTOR, Century Systems

1000 HRS - START-UP SCHEMES

Presentations will be made by the High Street banks, the Small Business Advisory Service and the British Franchise Association. Topics will include:

1 Capital

2 Loans

3 Development Boards

4 Government Schemes

5 Share Issues

6 Organisational Skills

There will also be a short talk from Mr Alan Stevenson who will advise on available help through various Government start-up schemes, eg financial assistance, administrational support etc.

1100 HRS - COFFEE

REF: OU/SH   2

Exercise 3A (continued)

Name   Exercise 3A   BUSINESS SEMINAR

1115 HRS - WHAT MAKES AN ENTREPRENEUR?

The speakers for each topic will lead a 45-minute debate on Income Tax, VAT and National Insurance. The aim is to make the participants more aware of the pitfalls and pleasures which come with self-employment.

With the aid of case histories, participants will be divided into groups and encouraged to discuss the viability of the respective businesses, types of business organisation, franchising, market research, and employment law.

The groups will then have an opportunity to put forward the main points from their discussions, including any particular questions which remain unanswered.

There will be a short 10-minute interval half-

way through this session.

1300 HRS - LUNCH IN 1ST FLOOR CARVERY

REF: OU/SH   3

Exercise 3A (continued)

Name Exercise 3A BUSINESS SEMINAR

<u>1400 HRS - CONSULTATION SESSIONS</u>

The 'experts' will make themselves available for individual consultation. Every participant can put forward his or her idea and receive, in return, valuable assistance along with constructive criticism.

There will be a short 10-minute interval half-

way through this session.

<u>1600 HRS - PLENARY SESSION/PRIZE PRESENTATION</u>

Adam Flynn, Marketing Director, will present an award - 'Business Idea of the Day' - together with a cheque for £175.00 to the 'entrepreneur' with the most original (and viable) business proposal.

(THE WINNER WILL BE CHOSEN BY THE PANEL OF EXPERTS

PRESENT AT THE SEMINAR.)

NB: Our offices are to be relocated in the West End Business Park, where our new, purpose-built accommodation is nearing completion. In the meantime, we are fortunate that we have been allowed to use the premises of the Stratton Hotel, High Street, for our Seminar.

REF: OU/SH 4

Exercise 3B

Name Exercise 3B EXHIBITION

A G O O D P L A C E T O W O R K ?

<u>An Exhibition for Office Workers</u>

The Information Technology revolution has changed our working lives and brought numerous benefits - both from the employer's point of view and the employees' angle. Although there are no serious occupational dangers (such as you might find in an engineering workshop or a foundry), there are still risks involved for those who work in an office environment.

<u>Managers/Supervisors</u> Do you know <u>exactly</u> what your responsibilities are under European Community legislation?

New government laws are now in effect which regulate the number of hours an operator may sit at a VDU without a break.

It is your job to assess the safe working order of every workstation in your section/department. It's up to you to make sure European Community recommendations are met.

<u>Electronic Office Workers/VDU Operators</u> If you suffer from eye strain, aching shoulders, back pain, headaches, you should ask the following questions:

1 What can you do to make your working day more comfortable?

2 How can your employer help?

3 Are you taking sufficient breaks away from the VDU screen?

4 Is the office furniture adequate, eg chair set to correct height and with a backrest?

5 Is the air-conditioning effective?

6 Have you had your eyesight checked by an optician since you started working on a VDU?

OFFICE WORKERS

Exercise 3B (continued)

Name Exercise 3B **EXHIBITION**

THERE WILL BE CONTINUOUS LECTURES ABOUT 3 AREAS OF INTEREST:

Health Eye problems, muscular strain, repetitive strain injury, VDUs and problems with pregnancy. Are all health problems really the computer's fault? What can be done to alleviate stress, strain and worry?

Ergonomics Workstations, systems, the workplace environment. It's usually easy to change some aspects such as chairs, desks, and lighting but it's more difficult to change the way we work and think!

This is a very extensive topic - you will be surprised what is involved.

Safety Electricity, radiation, chemicals. Expediency can lead to inadequate and dangerous practices in the use of electricity. There are many toxic chemicals in offices (but there's no risk provided due care is taken - 95% of accidents are caused through negligence). We'll give you the facts about radiation from VDUs.

2 OFFICE WORKERS

Exercise 3B (continued)

Name Exercise 3B **EXHIBITION**

THE EXHIBITION WILL OFFER:

1 Inter-active Video

2 Slides

3 Displays

4 Professional Advice from the many experts who will be on hand to deal with your individual problems

5 Quizzes, Questionnaires

There will also be an Information Stand offering advice on European Community legislation.

3 OFFICE WORKERS

Exercise 3B (continued)

Name Exercise 3B **EXHIBITION**

OPENING TIMES

Exhibition opens at 0930 hrs Monday - Saturday and closes at 1800 hrs Monday - Friday. (Early close Saturday 1600 hrs.)

Phone 071-124637 for exact location in your town - ask for Hamish Hamilton.

Admission fee: £1.00 Adults
£0.50 Children (accompanied)
£0.50 OAPs

Parties of 10 or more qualify for a 10% discount.

A G O O D P L A C E T O W O R K ?

An Exhibition for Office Workers

APPEARING SOON NEAR YOU!

4 OFFICE WORKERS

Exercise 4A

BURNDALE TERTIARY COLLEGE
Shaftesbury Road
BURNDALE
BE1 3WB

TEL NO (055) 375896
FAX NO (055) 623569

Date of typing Name EX4A

URGENT

Mrs U Adamson
Careers Teacher
Queen Anne's High School
Wellington Grove
BURNDALE
BE2 5AB

Dear Mrs Adamson

Visitors Day

I am writing to tell you about next week's Visitors Day at our College. Although it is rather short notice, I hope you will be able to attend, along with members of your staff and pupils. I must apologise for the letter's lateness; this is due to the fact that we have been waiting for the printing of our brochure and application forms, copies enclosed, to be completed.

The College will be open between the hours of 9 am and 7 pm on Thursday (next Thursday's date) and a buffet lunch will be served in the Training Restaurant for a limited number of careers teachers.

I am sending a copy of this letter to the Head of your 6th Form. Please return the enclosed form if you wish to join us for lunch - or telephone my secretary on Ext 3164 as soon as possible.

We believe the Visitors Day is an excellent opportunity for school pupils to get the information they require and to experience a day in the working life of the College. Pupils can view the accommodation and receive help and advice in selecting a course to suit them. The College Admissions Department will be available to make separate appointments for those pupils who wish to make a definite commitment to a full-time course.

Yours sincerely

M J CRABTREE
Marketing Officer, Burndale Tertiary College

Encs

Copy to Head of 6th Form, Queen Anne's High School

Exercise 4B

Exercise 4B

BURNDALE TERTIARY COLLEGE
Shaftesbury Road
BURNDALE BE1 3WB

B U S I N E S S   A D M I N I S T R A T I O N

<u>Full-time Courses</u>

Business Administration courses are related to National Vocational Qualifications (NVQs) at levels 2, 3 and 4. Students follow a programme based on their previous experience and qualifications, and designed to meet each individual's needs. All courses run for 1 year but may be extended to 2 years for those who wish to improve their job prospects and qualifications.

Our courses provide an excellent starting point for a career in the business world. The skills learned can be transferred to many different jobs at different levels - from office junior to managing director.

<u>The Business Administration Programme</u>

The core subjects are:

Typewriting
Word Processing
Computer Applications

The timetable is organized in such a way that students can then choose additional options from the following list:

Shorthand	Book-keeping
Audio-typewriting	European Studies
German for Business*	French for Business*
Desk Top Publishing	Statistics for Business*

* A GCSE grade A-C in the relevant language is necessary in order to begin studying languages for business, and in mathematics for statistics for business.

1

Exercise 4B (continued)

Name Exercise 4B

<u>Practical Experience</u>

The majority of the work is practical in nature and students work at their own pace. Work placements are a valuable part of all our courses. Students work in local businesses for 3 weeks - 1 week per term in a 3-term course.

<u>How to Apply</u>

An application form may be completed at any time - not just during the Spring and Summer terms. It can be a definite advantage to apply early as the courses are popular. Forms should be received by the Admissions Officer, Jenny McEwan, by the end of June so that preliminary interviews can be organized. However, late applications are very welcome. It's never too late!

<u>Commencement of Courses</u>

The courses will begin on Monday 9 September at 9.00 am. Attendance is from 9.00 am to 5.00 pm each day except Wednesday when the afternoon is left free for leisure/creative pursuits.

COME TO OUR VISITORS DAY

<u>Thursday (correct date inserted)</u>

9.00 am - 7.00 pm

2

Exercise 4C

Name   Exercise 4C

BA/COURSES

BURNDALE TERTIARY COLLEGE
Shaftesbury Road
BURNDALE   BE1 3WB

<u>COURSES IN BUSINESS ADMINISTRATION</u>

FULL-TIME COURSES

Business Administration courses are centred around National Vocational Qualifications (NVQs) at levels 2, 3 and 4. Students follow a 'modular' programme, the structure of which is based on their previous experience and qualifications. All courses run for 1 year from September - June but may be extended to 2 years for those who wish to improve their job prospects with advanced qualifications.

Our courses provide an excellent basis for a career in the world of business. The skills learned can be transferred to many different jobs at different levels - from Office Junior to Managing Director.

COME TO OUR VISITORS DAY

<u>Thursday (correct date inserted)</u>

9.00 am - 7.00 pm

Exercise 4C (continued)

Name   Exercise 4C

BA/COURSES

THE BUSINESS ADMINISTRATION PROGRAMME

The core subjects are:

Typewriting	Office Administration
Word Processing	Computer Applications

The timetable is organised in such a way that students can then choose additional options from the following list:

Shorthand	Book-keeping
Audio-typewriting	European Studies
German for Business*	French for Business*
Desk Top Publishing	Statistics for Business*

* A GCSE grade A-C in German or French is necessary in order to begin studying languages for business, and in mathematics for 'Statistics for Business'.

PRACTICAL EXPERIENCE

The majority of the training is practical in nature and students work at their own pace. Work experience is a valuable part of all our courses. Students carry out 'real work' in local businesses for 3 weeks - 1 week per term in a 3-term course.

In the past, we have (wherever possible) organised a different work placement for each of the 3 weeks.

The College is proud of its technology, eg 3 rooms of new up-to-date computers, 2 colour laser printers and a range of industry-standard software packages.

PAGE NO 2

Exercise 4C (continued)

Name   Exercise 4C

BA/COURSES

PART-TIME COURSES

We offer a wide range of part-time courses whether in single subjects (eg typewriting, word processing, shorthand) and also in Business Administration NVQ Levels 2 and 3. Some examples of these are listed below:

PAGE NO 3

Exercise 4C (continued)

Name   Exercise 4C

BA/COURSES

COMMENCEMENT OF COURSES

All full-time courses commence on Monday 9 September at 9.00 am.

Enrolment dates for part-time courses are available from the College Reception and are also published 2 weeks prior to commencement in the local press.

HOW TO APPLY

An application form may be completed at any time. It can be a definite advantage to apply early as the courses are popular. Application forms for full-time courses should be received by the Admissions Officer, Jenny McEwan, by the end of June so that preliminary interviews can be organised. However, late applications are very welcome. It's never too late!

COME TO OUR VISITORS DAY

<u>Thursday (correct date inserted)</u>

9.00 am - 7.00 pm

PAGE NO 4

Exercise 5A

J U N I O R   M E M B E R S H I P   F O R M

Jo-Jo Junior Dance Team

Membership No *

Surname *

First Name *

Address *

Tel No *

Age *

Date of Birth *

Sex *

Attending: JAZZ - Monday
MODERN DANCE - Wednesday
BALLET - Friday
CREATIVE DANCE - Saturday

(please tick sessions to be attended)

Fee Paid *

Date of Joining *

Exercise 5B

TELEPHONE MESSAGE

ACTION: URGENT/NON-URGENT
RING BACK
WILL CALL AGAIN LATER

MESSAGE FOR ....

DATE .... TIME ....

CALLER'S NAME ....

CALLER'S COMPANY ....

CALLER'S TEL NO ....

MESSAGE ....

....

....

....

Received by .... Date ....

Exercise 6C

SILSTON SUMMER FESTIVAL

EVENT TIME		DISPLAY TEAM	EVENT NAME	NAME OF ORGANISER	ARENA
START	END				
JUNIOR SECTION					
1400	1430	JAY DANCEBIRDS	Sun and Wind[1]	June Berry	1
1435	1500	FARRAH SINGERS	Junior Medley	Ann Shaw	1
1505	1525	JAY DANCEBIRDS	Dreams and Destinies	June Berry	1
1400	1500	FARRAH GYM SQUAD	Gymnastics	Mark Drew	2
1505	1525	DANCE MINORS	Sugar and Spice	Maria Lee	2
1400	1445	SILSTON CHOIR	Yankee Doodle Dandy	Alan Green	3
1455	1525	FARRAH SINGERS	Southern Belle	Ann Shaw	3
ADULT SECTION					
1530	1630	LAVELL DANCERS	Jazz American	Sue Vine	1
1645	1745	SILSTON CHOIR	Copacabana	Alan Green	1
1530	1600	FARRAH SINGERS	Adult Medley	Ann Shaw	2
1610	1630	THE DEVETTES	Guitar Duet[2]	Jo Devette	2
1645	1745	SILSTON BAND	Brass Bonanza	Paul Knell	2
1530	1630	SILSTON BAND	City Lights	Paul Knell	3
1645	1745	SILSTON CHOIR	Showboat	Alan Green	3

1 A mixture of classical ballet, jazz and contemporary dance music over the last century

2 Speciality act featuring Spanish Flamenco guitar and Spanish dancing by the Jay Dancebirds

Exercise 6B

NEW RANGE OF DEVANE PRODUCTS

ADDITIONS TO THE CATALOGUE

CAT REF NO	STOCK DESCRIPTION	SIZE	COST[1]		PAGE
			-10	10+	
QW3	Devane Leather Briefcase	18x13x5 in	£39.99	£35.99	2
QW5	Devane Writing Case[2]	8x7x1 in	£17.99	£16.99	3
QW7	Devane Executive Case	18x13x5 in	£49.99	£45.99	5
QW8	Devane Attache Case	18x13x4 in	£59.99	£53.99	6

1 Bulk orders of 50+ qualify for a further discount.

2 Available in black, red or green.

Exercise 7A

Mrs P Waterston
12 Oak Drive
Netherton
EDGERTON
EN5 9OL
Mrs Waterston
Veteran

Mr M E Willson
26 Fairway
ROYDEN
RN6 4JL
Mr Willson
Veteran

Mrs M Horsfall
18 Lea Road
Leafield
BROOK HILL
BK7 2HK
Mrs Horsfall
Veteran

Ms V Varley
4 Water Lane
NORFIELD
ND16 8LL
Ms Varley
Ordinary

Mr I K Thompson
26 Summer Close
Sunley
LANGTON
LN9 6EJ
Mr Thompson
Ordinary

Exercise 7A (continued)

Name Exercise 7A (Standard letter)

Today's date

(Code for ADDRESS field)

Dear ***(Code for SALUTATION field)***

I am pleased to be able to tell you that the event which has been organised for our spring run is open to ***(Code for VARIABLE field)*** members. Please contact me if you would like further details.

Yours sincerely

James Stevens
Events Organiser

Exercise 7A (continued)

Name Exercise 7A

Today's date

Mrs M Horsfall
18 Lea Road
Leafield
BROOK HILL
BK7 2HK

Dear Mrs Horsfall

I am pleased to be able to tell you that the event which has been organised for our spring run is open to Veteran members. Please contact me if you would like further details.

Yours sincerely

James Stevens
Events Organiser

==

<u>LETTERS ALSO TO:</u>   **Mrs P Waterston and Mr M E Willson**

Exercise 7B

Name Exercise 7B (Datafile)

Mrs J Brookner
36 Windsor Road
Wooldale
HUDDERSFIELD
HD7 8WB
Mrs Brookner
Jazz Adult

Mr E Dale
125 Newton Hill
BRIGHOUSE
HD6 3ME
Mr Dale
Creative Junior

Mr O Kozlowski
147 Kirkstone Avenue
Highley
BRIGHOUSE
HD6 2BE
Mr Kozlowski
Jazz Junior

Ms R E Rose
14 Wykeham Rise
KEIGHLEY
BD22 5DD
Ms Rose
Creative Junior

Ms L Knight
Thorn View
Kirkwood
HUDDERSFIELD
HD6 9DH
Ms Knight
Jazz Junior

Mr B Brown
10 Sandy Hill Lane
SOWERBY BRIDGE
HX3 3PO
Mr Brown
Jazz Junior

Mr P M Robinson
151 Meadow Grove
Kirkwood
HUDDERSFIELD
HD6 4HM
Mr Robinson
Creative Adult

Exercise 7B (continued)

(Date of typing)

<u>(Code for ADDRESS field)</u>

Dear <u>(Code for SALUTATION field)</u>

NORTHERN JUNIOR JAZZ DUO COMPETITION

The annual competition will take place as usual at Milltown Civic Centre on Saturday 2 May. For the past few years, we have entered between 4 and 6 couples and, last year, Gary Murphy and Anna Mayman of our Club were winners in the Under-13 section.

As a regular attender at our <u>(Code for VARIABLE field)</u> sessions, I would like to invite you to enter the competition and I enclose an application form. Please complete and return this to me as soon as possible giving the name of your proposed partner.

Further information and details about our special competition training sessions can be obtained from Mary Steward.

Yours sincerely

Michelle Woodman
MEMBERSHIP SECRETARY

Enc

Exercise 7B (continued)

(Date of typing)

Ms L Knight
Thorn View
Kirkwood
HUDDERSFIELD
HD6 9DH

Dear Ms Knight

NORTHERN JUNIOR JAZZ DUO COMPETITION

The annual competition will take place as usual at Milltown Civic Centre on Saturday 2 May. For the past few years, we have entered between 4 and 6 couples and, last year, Gary Murphy and Anna Mayman of our Club were winners in the Under-13 section.

As a regular attender at our Jazz Junior sessions, I would like to invite you to enter the competition and I enclose an application form. Please complete and return this to me as soon as possible giving the name of your proposed partner.

Further information and details about our special competition training sessions can be obtained from Mary Steward.

Yours sincerely

Michelle Woodman
MEMBERSHIP SECRETARY

Enc

==

<u>LETTERS ALSO TO:</u>   **Mr B Brown and Mr O Kozlowski**

Exercise 7C

Mrs C Beaty
16 Tennyson Drive
BACKWOOD
BD4 7MA
Cathy
Branch 1 Personnel

Mr A L Brearley
Bridge End
BROWNSHAW
BW9 3AB
Adrian
Branch 1 Personnel

Mrs W Cawdwell
10 Dean Cottages
Deanshaw
HIGH WELLS
HS3 3NB
Wendy
Branch 2 Personnel

Mr A K Basu
6 Hill View Drive
Carr Hill
BROWNSHAW
BW3 4HA
Asoke
Branch 1 Personnel

Ms A Forder
18 Thomas Street
Southwood
BACKWOOD
BD6 7LJ
Alison
Branch 3 Personnel

Miss L Lord
10 Overwood Lane
Overwood
LONSDALE
LE9 6SN
Lynda
Branch 1 Personnel

Miss S Hussain
29 Nelson Avenue
Renshaw
RAWTON
RN6 8JL
Shahena
Branch 1 Accounts

Miss J L Stocks
Birch View
BACKWOOD
BD10 4LM
Jenny
Branch 1 Personnel

Mrs C Lefevre
16 Lindon Way
RAWTON
RN5 7LM
Claire
Branch 1 Purchasing

Mr H Fischer
16 Trafford Close
Merevale
HIGH WELLS
HS4 9LW
Helmut
Branch 1 Personnel

Exercise 7C (continued)

(Date of typing)

(Code for ADDRESS field)

Dear (Code for SALUTATION field)

HUMAN RESOURCE MANAGEMENT - CURRENT ISSUES

The Company is holding training sessions over the coming 6 months and I would like to invite you to attend. I am writing to all staff employed in (Code for VARIABLE field). I hope you will consider the proposed sessions relevant to your day-to-day work. It is our policy to keep abreast of new developments in current practice and to apply new ideas in a practical way with the complete involvement of staff at all levels.

The sessions will run for 2 or 3 days, depending on the content, and accomodation will be provided. The following venues will be used:

BIRMINGHAM
LEEDS
GLASGOW
ABERDEEN
NEWCASTLE
BRISTOL
LONDON
BELFAST

Attendance will be at the discretion of your Section Manager with whom you should discuss your interest. I enclose full details of the various courses and an application form. Please return your completed form to your Section Manager.

I look forward to seeing you at one of the above venues.

Yours sincerely
PERFECT BUILDING SOCIETY

M D TRAVIS
Personnel Director

Encs

Exercise 7C (continued)

(Date of typing)

Mr A K Basu
6 Hill View Drive
Carr Hill
BROWNSHAW
BW3 4HA

Dear Asoke

HUMAN RESOURCE MANAGEMENT - CURRENT ISSUES

The Company is holding training sessions over the coming 6 months and I would like to invite you to attend. I am writing to all staff employed in Branch 1 Personnel. I hope you will consider the proposed sessions relevant to your day-to-day work. It is our policy to keep abreast of new developments in current practice and to apply new ideas in a practical way with the complete involvement of staff at all levels.

The sessions will run for 2 or 3 days, depending on the content, and accommodation will be provided. The following venues will be used:

BIRMINGHAM
LEEDS
GLASGOW
ABERDEEN
NEWCASTLE
BRISTOL
LONDON
BELFAST

Attendance will be at the discretion of your Section Manager with whom you should discuss your interest. I enclose full details of the various courses and an application form. Please return your completed form to your Section Manager.

I look forward to seeing you at one of the above venues.

Yours sincerely
PERFECT BUILDING SOCIETY

M D TRAVIS
Personnel Director

Encs

==

LETTERS ALSO TO:	**Mr A L Brearley**	**Mr A K Basu**
	Miss L Lord	**Miss J L Stocks**
	Mr H Fischer	

Exercise 8A

A P P L I C A T I O N   F O R M

Company Weekend Excursion

Excursion A: PARIS .....

Excursion B: AMSTERDAM .....

Excursion C: VIENNA .....

(please tick choice required)

Surname ....

Forenames ....

Address ....

....

Date of Birth ....

Payroll No .... Department ....

No of Adult Places Required ....

No of Child Places Required ....

I apply for a total of .... places for the above excursion. I agree to abide by the company rules and regulations for the duration of the excursion.

Signed .... Date ....

(NB: Line draw not mandatory)

Exercise 8B

COMPANY WEEKEND EXCURSION

The following personnel are to be included on the 3 company weekend excursions. Coaches for all excursions will depart from Head Office on Friday 26 September at 1330 hours, and return Monday 29 September at 2230 hours.

CODE	EMPLOYEE NAME	PAYROLL NUMBER	TICKETS REQUIRED		TOTAL COST £
			ADULT	CHILD	
EXCURSION TO PARIS - 90[1]					
A	Elizabeth Brant	22563	2	2	270.00
A	Alexandria Ferry	34112	4	1	405.00
A	Mark Goodwill	33441	2	4	360.00
A	Jonathan Kettle	22478	2	3	315.00
EXCURSION TO AMSTERDAM - 110[2]					
B	Grahame Dilling	22672	2	1	286.00
B	Francesca Hollins	23235	2	0	220.00
B	Brian McIntosh	31889	3	0	330.00
EXCURSION TO VIENNA - 135.00[3]					
C	Matthew Jay	39110	2	0	270.00
C	Margaret Pendle	27610	2	0	270.00
C	Susannah Wharfe	34447	2	2	540.00

1 **Child discount 50% (same discount for OAPs)**

2 **Child discount 40%**

3 **No discount available on this excursion.**

Exercise 8C

DATA8

Mrs P Grant
Grattan & Moore Ltd
12-15 Cornfield Street
BRADFORD
BD3 4NF
Mrs Grant
11 July - 15 July

Mr M Akram
Greaves Bros Ltd
Slade Street
HALIFAX
HX2 3ES
Mr Akram
11 August - 15 August

Mrs J Baines
Vale Components PLC
Vale Mill
DEWSBURY
WF10 5MP
Mrs Baines
11 July - 15 July

Mr S E Pedlipska
Pedlipska Plant Hire Ltd
Hollinwell Works
KEIGHLEY
BD22 1HP
Mr Pedlipska
21 July - 25 July

Miss K M Bolton
Birkby Signs Ltd
Birkby Lane West
CLECKHEATON
CN9 6BD
Miss Bolton
11 July - 15 July

Ms Y Wigglesworth
Outwood Electrics PLC
Royd Mill
LIVERSEDGE
BD13 3RS
Ms Wigglesworth
11 July - 15 July

Mrs S Saddique
Long & James Ltd
16 Melbury Road
SOWERBY BRIDGE
HX3 1EL
Mrs Pellon
11 August - 15 August

Mr M N Neocleous
Hellenic Foods
Valley Business Park
BRIGHOUSE
HD5 2AU
Mr Neocleous
21 August - 25 August

Mr K Firth
Firth Kitchens Ltd
West Road Mill
HUDDERSFIELD
HD2 7SF
Mr Firth
11 July - 15 July

Mrs P A House
Newall Products Ltd
Paddock Avenue
SKIPTON
BD30 4DD
Mrs House
11 July - 15 July

Exercise 8C (continued)

LETT8

(Date of typing)

[Code for ADDRESS field]

Dear *[Code for SALUTATION field]*

Northern News Weekend Breaks

Thank you for contacting me about our new excursions programme.

I note that you would be interested in arranging a break in Amsterdam for employees at your Company for the dates of *[Code for VARIABLE field]*, and I have pleasure in enclosing full details.

The Hotel Parador will be our base for the weekend.

As you can see from the photograph, it is a large, modern hotel with a wide range of amenities. (Colour leaflets are enclosed.)

The cost per person will be £210 and this includes travel from and to Leeds, accommodation on a bed and breakfast basis, and insurance. Parties of 12 and over attract the privilege of one free place for the organiser.

Please telephone me as soon as possible if you wish to make a definite reservation as demand is proving to be unexpectedly high.

Yours faithfully
NORTHERN NEWS

M Hickson
Travel Manager

Encs

Exercise 8C (continued)

MERG8

(Date of typing)

Mrs P Grant
Grattan & Moore Ltd
12-15 Cornfield Street
BRADFORD
BD3 4NF

Dear Mrs Grant

Northern News Weekend Breaks

Thank you for contacting me about our new excursions programme.

I note that you would be interested in arranging a break in Amsterdam for employees at your Company for the dates of 11 July - 15 July, and I have pleasure in enclosing full details.

The Hotel Parador will be our base for the weekend.

As you can see from the photograph, it is a large, modern hotel with a wide range of amenities. (Colour leaflets are enclosed.)

The cost per person will be £210 and this includes travel from and to Leeds, accommodation on a bed and breakfast basis, and insurance. Parties of 12 and over attract the privilege of one free place for the organiser.

Please telephone me as soon as possible if you wish to make a definite reservation as demand is proving to be unexpectedly high.

Yours faithfully
NORTHERN NEWS

M Hickson
Travel Manager

Encs

LETTERS ALSO TO:		
	Mrs J S Baines	**Miss K M Bolton**
	Ms Y Wigglesworth	**Mr K Firth**
	Mrs P A House	